EASY PIANO

MOTOWN HITS

ISBN 0-634-00013-6

HAL•LEONARD®
CORPORATION
7777 W. BLUEMOUND RD. P.O. BOX 13819 MILWAUKEE, WI 53213

Visit Hal Leonard Online at
www.halleonard.com

ABC

Words and Music by ALPHONSO MIZELL,
FREDERICK PERREN, DEKE RICHARDS
and BERRY GORDY

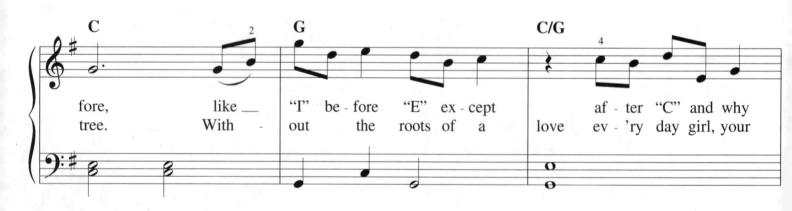

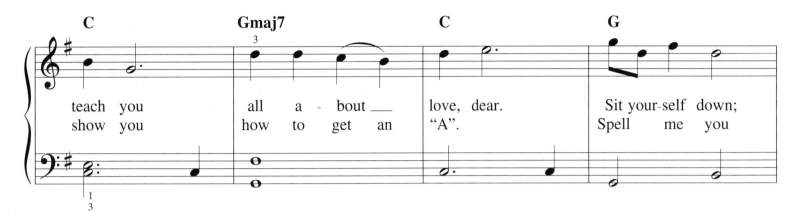

teach you / all a - bout ___ / love, dear. / Sit your-self down;
show you / how to get an / "A". / Spell me you

take a seat; / all you got - ta do is re - / peat af - ter me: ___
add the two, / lis - ten to me ba - by, that's / all you got - ta do.

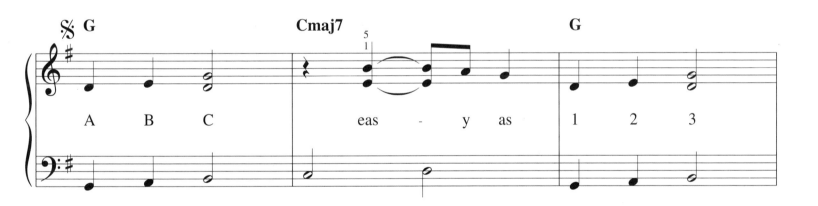

A B C / eas - y as / 1 2 3

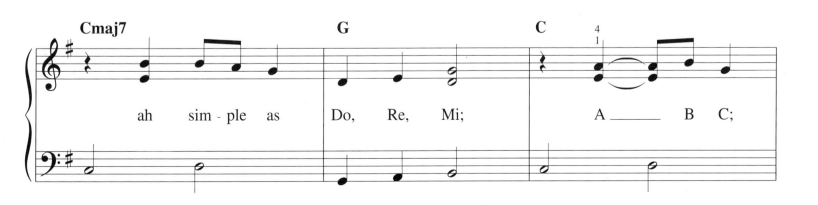

ah sim - ple as / Do, Re, Mi; / A ___ B C;

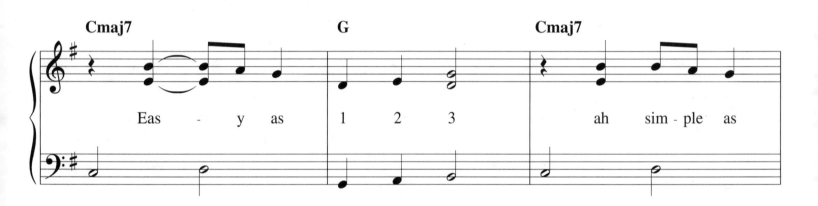

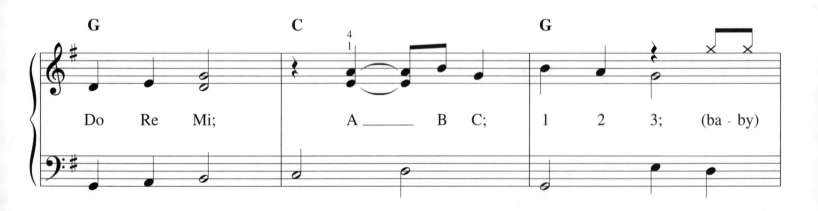

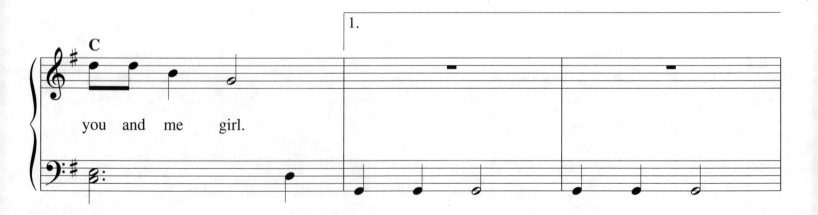

Come on, let me love you just a lit - tle bit;

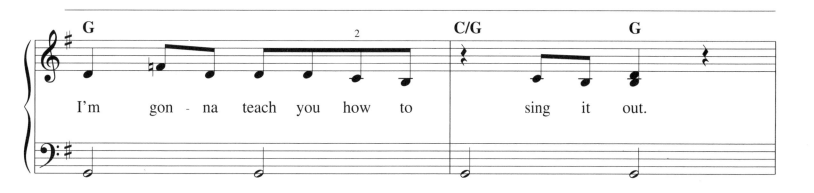

I'm gon - na teach you how to sing it out.

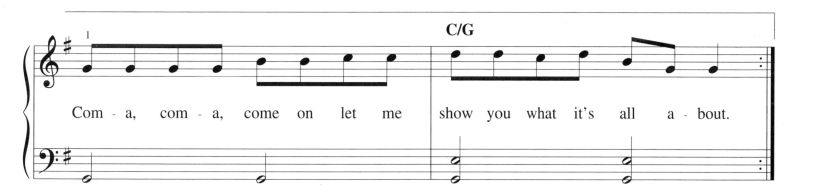

Com - a, com - a, come on let me show you what it's all a - bout.

Yah

sit down girl

I think I love you.

No get up girl show me what you can do.

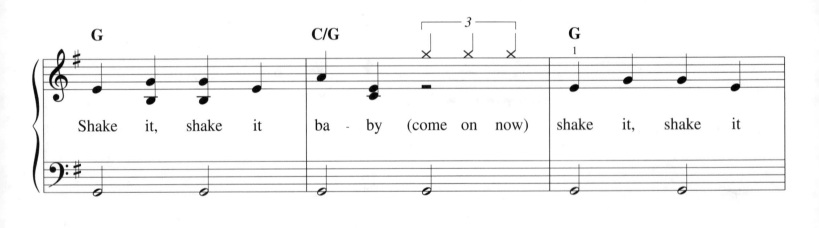

Shake it, shake it ba - by (come on now) shake it, shake it

D.S. and Fade

ba - by, oo, shake it, shake it ba - by (hey.)

BABY LOVE

Words and Music by BRIAN HOLLAND,
EDWARD HOLLAND and LAMONT DOZIER

8

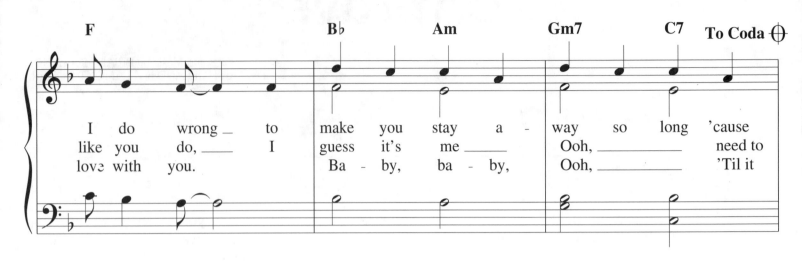

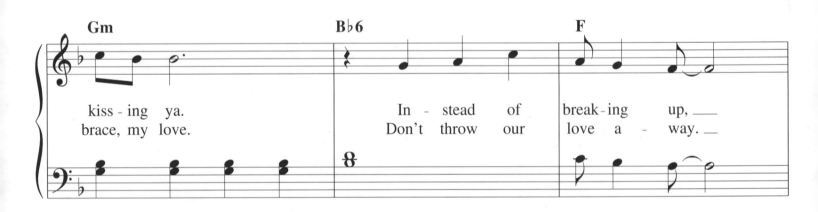

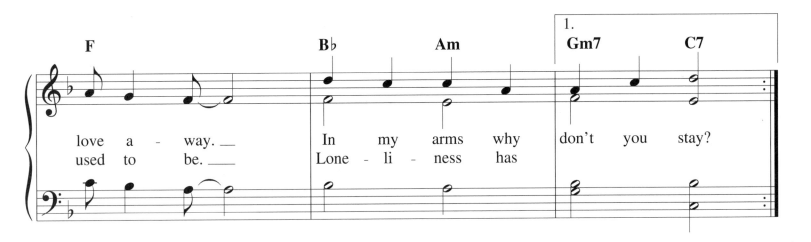

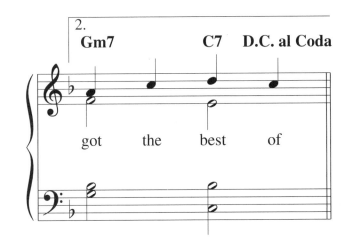

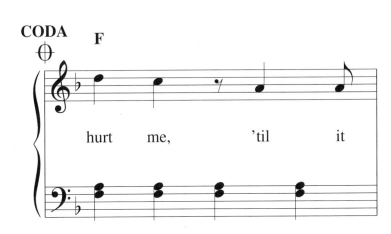

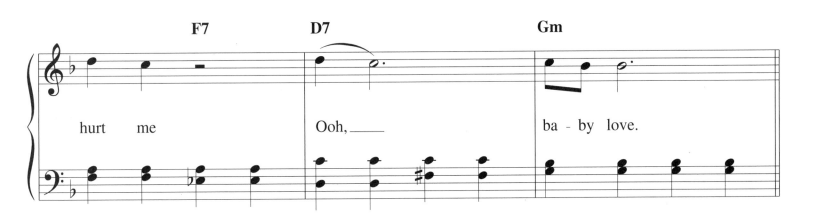

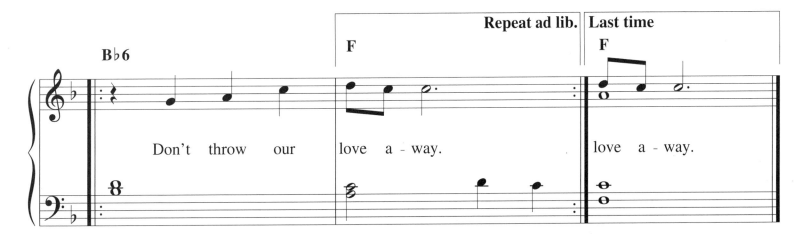

BEN

Words by DON BLACK
Music by WALTER SCHARF

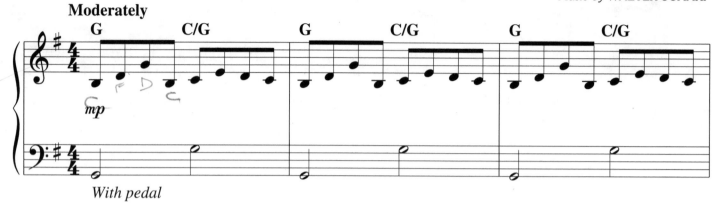

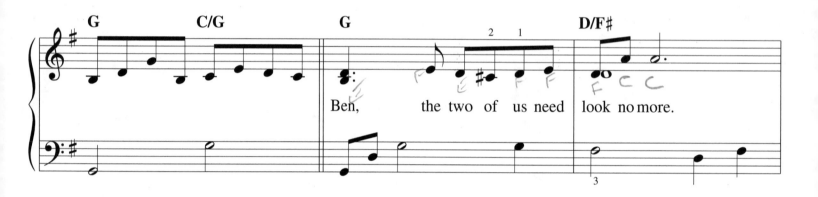

Ben, the two of us need look no more.

We both found what we were look-ing for. With a friend to call my

own, I'll nev-er be a-lone, and you, my friend, will see, you've got a friend in

me.

Ben, you're al-ways run-ning here and there. You feel you're not want-ed

an-y-where. If you ev-er look be-hind and don't like what you

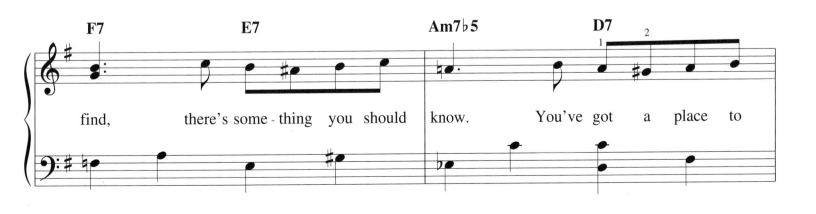

find, there's some-thing you should know. You've got a place to

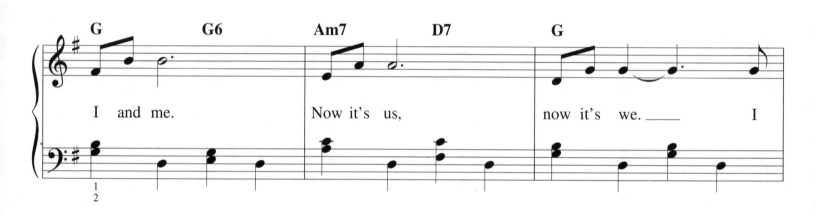

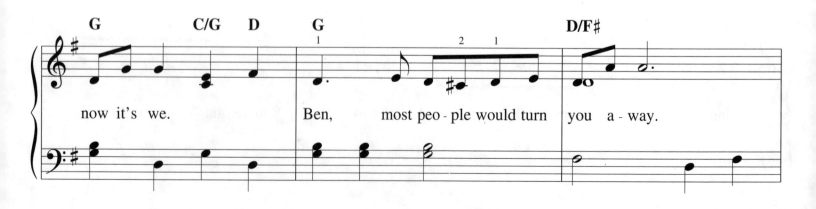

I don't lis-ten to a word they say. They don't see you as I

do; I wish they would try to. I'm sure they'd think a - gain if they had a friend like

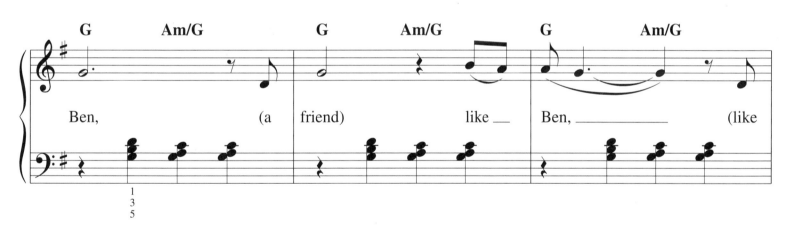

Ben, (a friend) like __ Ben, _____ (like

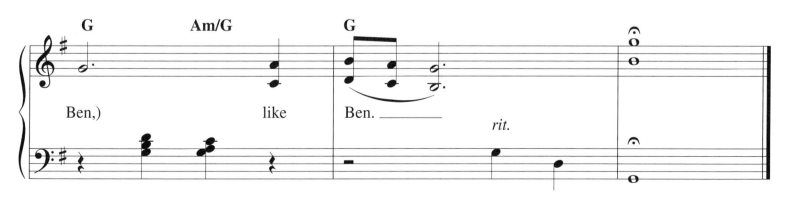

Ben,) like Ben. _____ *rit.*

COME SEE ABOUT ME

Words and Music by LAMONT DOZIER,
BRIAN HOLLAND and EDWARD HOLLAND

Moderately, with a beat

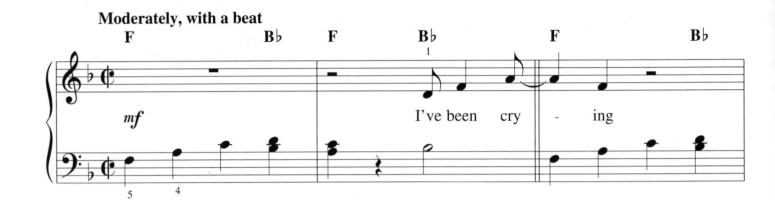

I've been cry - ing

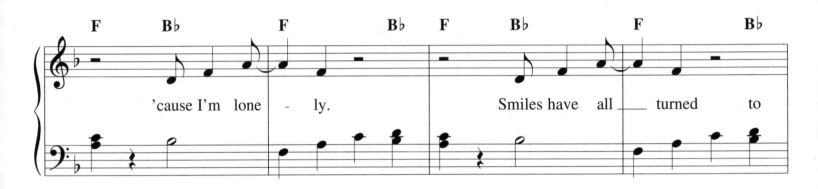

'cause I'm lone - ly. Smiles have all _ turned to

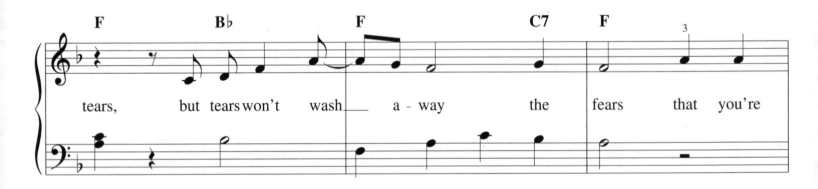

tears, but tears won't wash _ a - way the fears that you're

nev - er, ev - er gon - na turn _ to ease the fire _ that with - in me
mat - ter what you do or say _ I'm gon - na love you an - y -

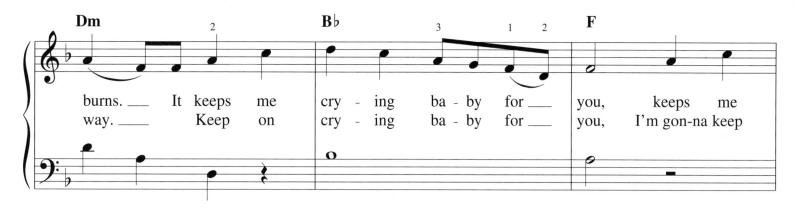

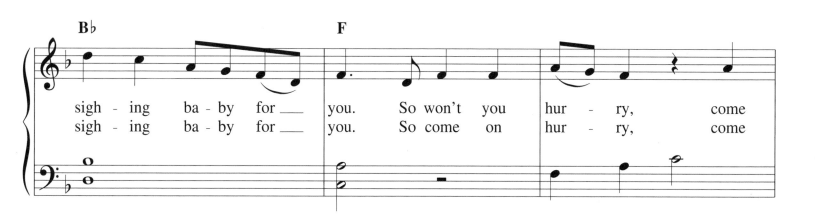

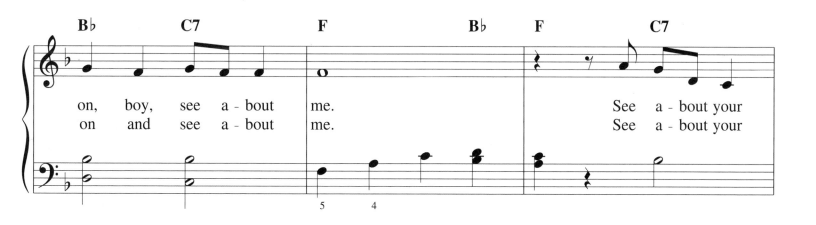

you have too. No peace shall I find un-til you come

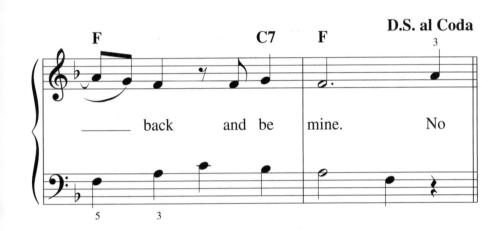

back and be mine. No

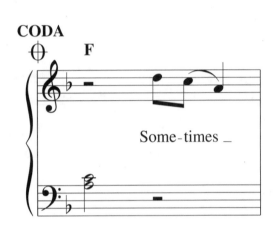

Some-times

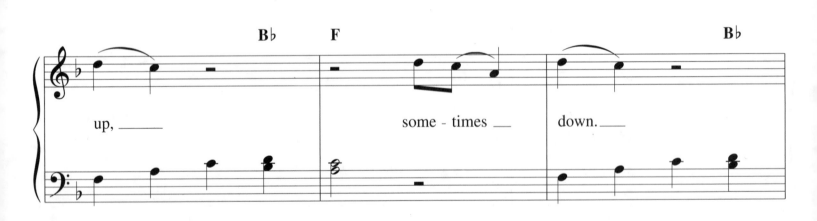

up, some - times down.

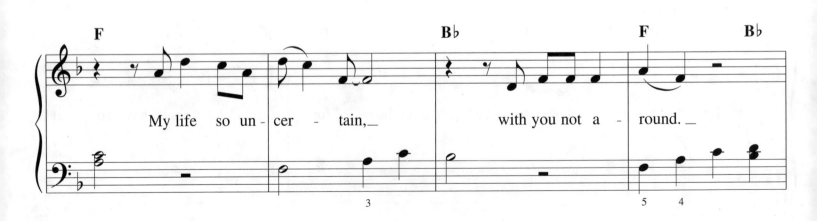

My life so un-cer - tain, with you not a - round.

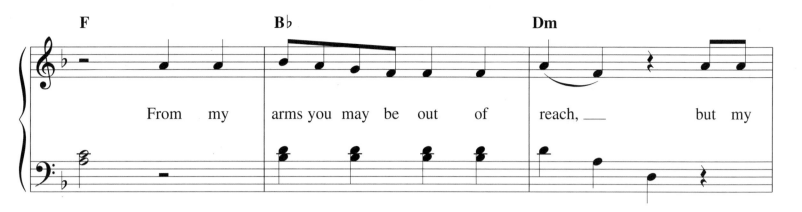

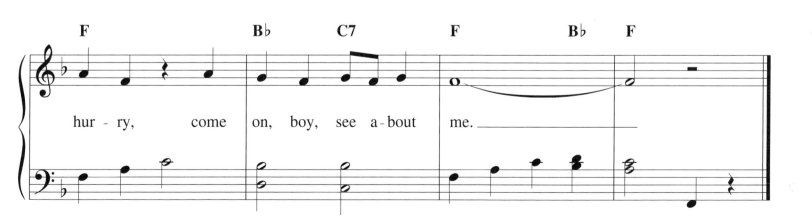

DANCING IN THE STREET

Words and Music by MARVIN GAYE,
IVY HUNTER and WILLIAM STEVENSON

Moderately bright

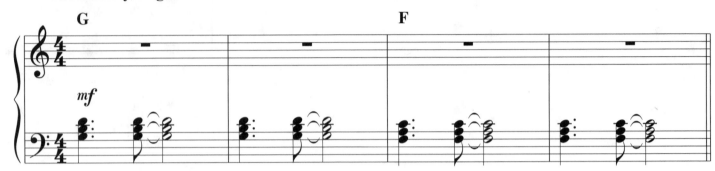

Call-ing out a-round the world, are you read-y for a brand new beat?
in-vi-ta-tion a-cross the na-tion a chance for the folks to meet.

There'll be Sum-mer's here, and the time is right for
laugh-in', sing-in', mu-sic swing-in', and

swing-ing and sway - ing, and re-cords play - ing, they're danc - in' ___ in the street. ___

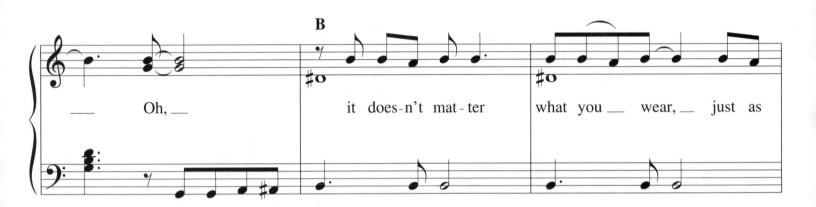

___ Oh, ___ it does-n't mat - ter what you ___ wear, ___ just as

long as you are there. ___ So come on, ev - 'ry guy ___

grab a girl, ___ ev - 'ry - where ___ a - round the world, ___ there'll be

danc - in'._____ There's danc - in' in the street.___

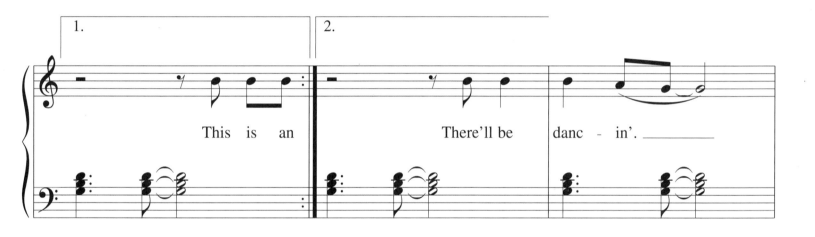

1.   2.

This is an   There'll be   danc - in'._____

There's danc-in' in the street.__

EASY

Words and Music by
LIONEL RICHIE

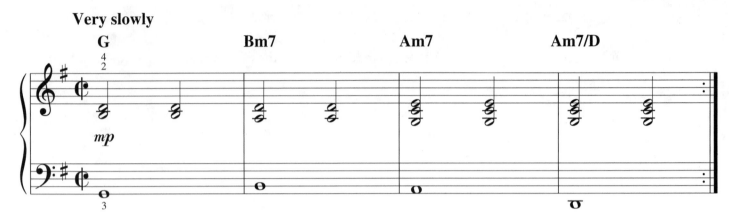

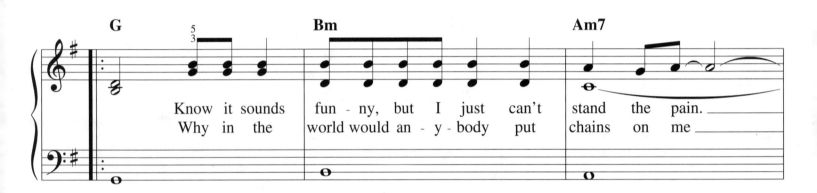

Know it sounds fun - ny, but I just can't stand the pain. ___
Why in the world would an - y - body put chains on me ___

Girl, I'm leav - ing you ___ to - mor - row. ___
I've paid my dues ___ to make it. ___

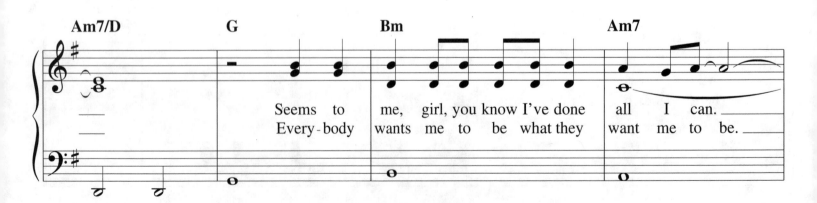

Seems to me, girl, you know I've done all I can. ___
Every - body wants me to be what they want me to be. ___

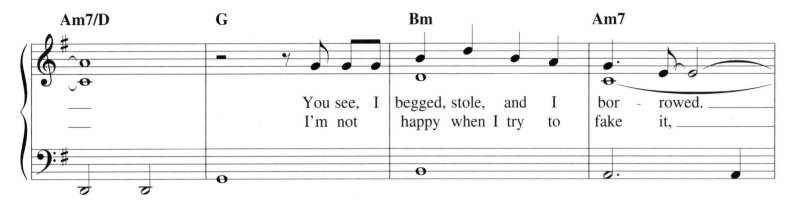

You see, I begged, stole, and I bor - rowed.
I'm not happy when I try to fake it,

Yeah, ___ ooh. ___ That's why I'm eas - y,
no, ___ ooh. ___

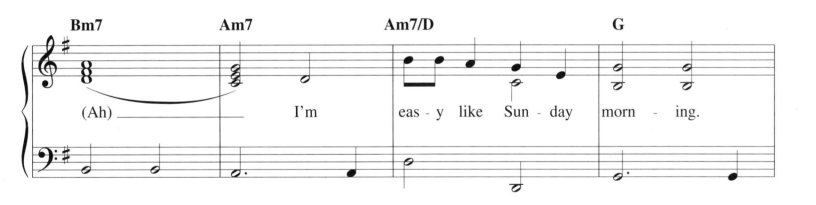

(Ah) ___ I'm eas - y like Sun - day morn - ing.

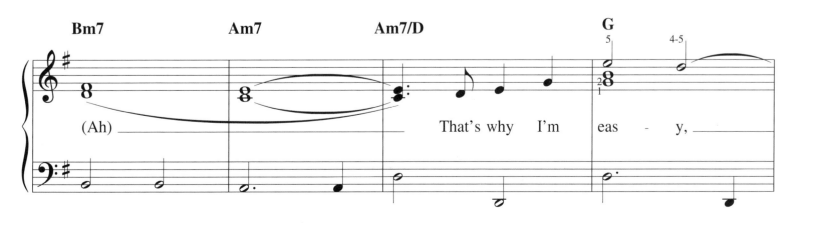

(Ah) ___ That's why I'm eas - y,

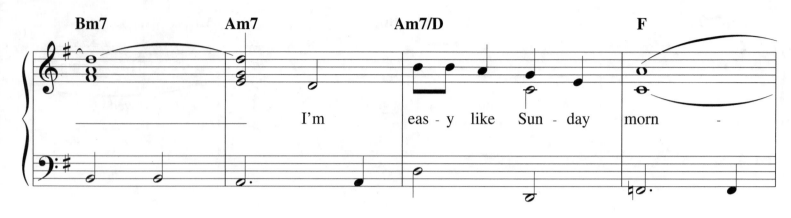

I'm eas-y like Sun-day morn -

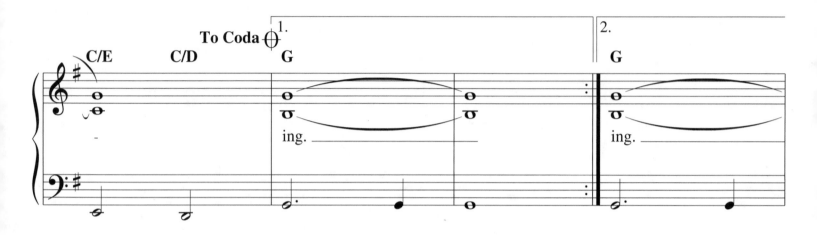

ing. ing.

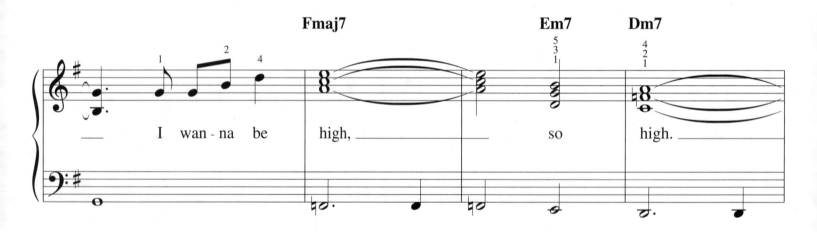

I wan-na be high, so high.

I wan-na be free to know the things I do are

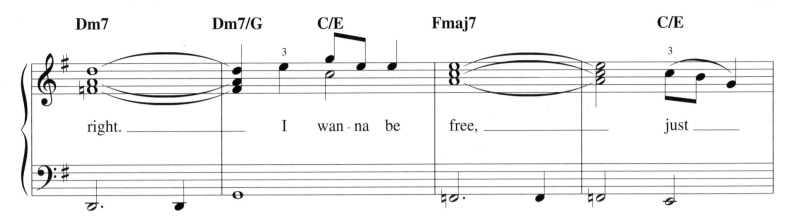

right. _____ I wan-na be free, _____ just _____

me, oh, _____ babe...

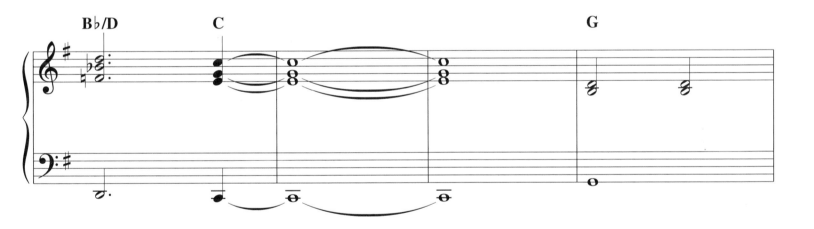

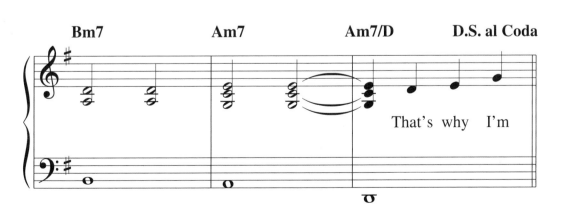

That's why I'm

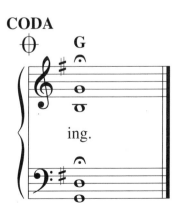

ing.

HEATWAVE
(Love Is Like a Heatwave)

Words and Music by EDWARD HOLLAND,
LAMONT DOZIER and BRIAN HOLLAND

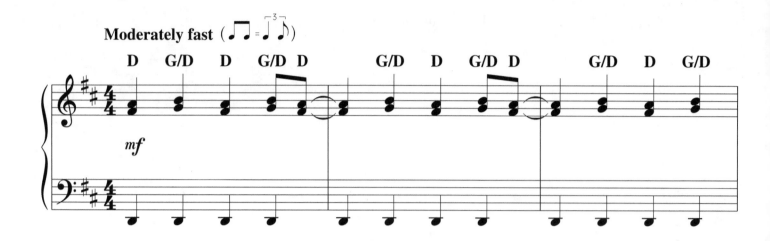

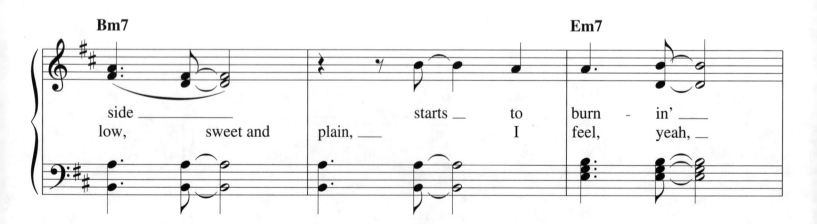

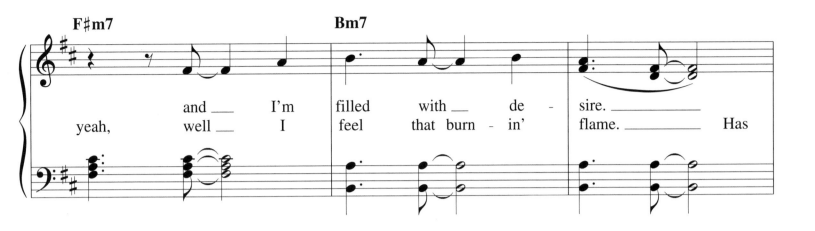

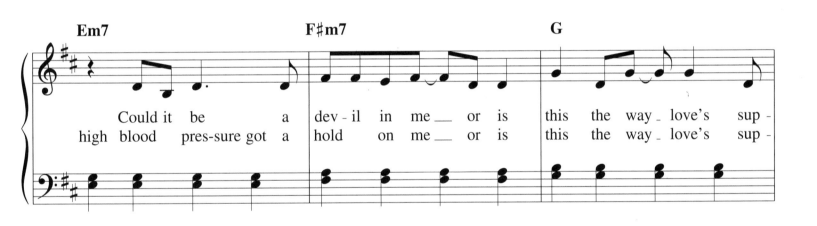

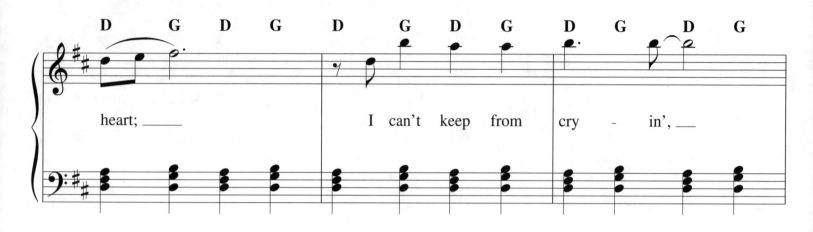

heart; _____ I can't keep from cry - in', ___

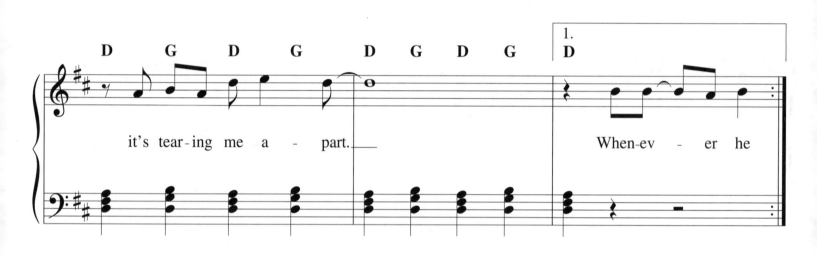

it's tear-ing me a - part. ___ When-ev - er he

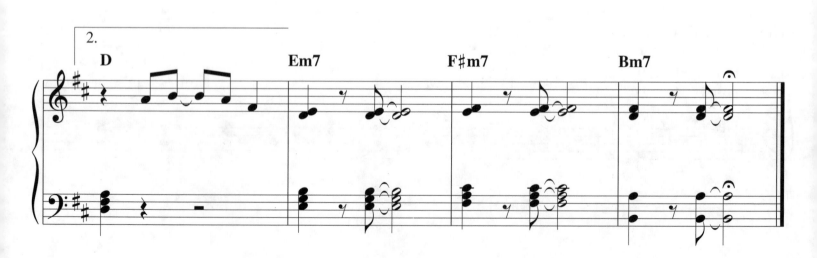

I CAN'T HELP MYSELF
(Sugar Pie, Honey Bunch)

Words and Music by BRIAN HOLLAND,
LAMONT DOZIER and EDWARD HOLLAND

Moderately fast

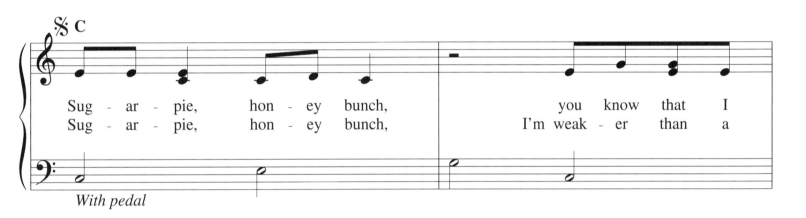

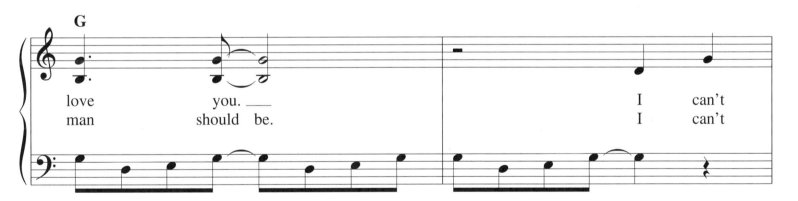

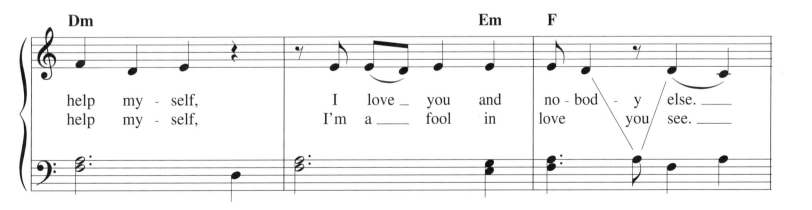

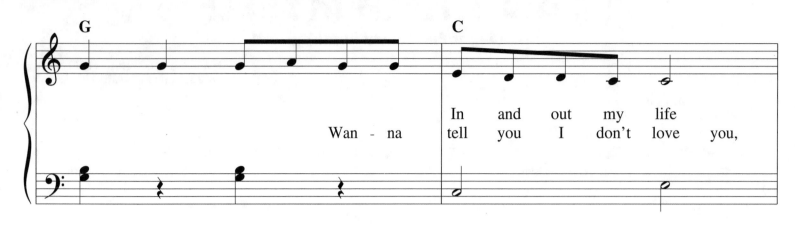

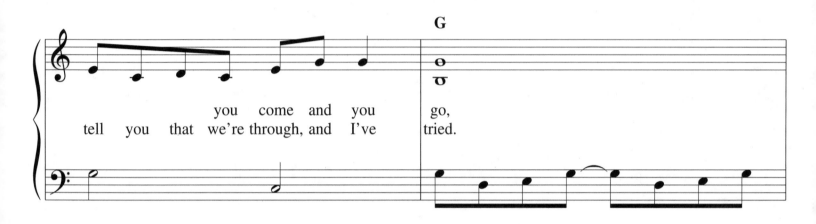

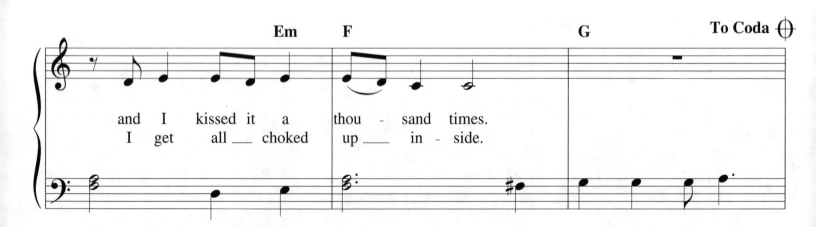

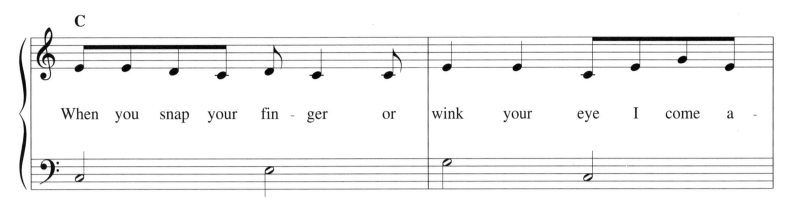

When you snap your fin - ger or wink your eye I come a -

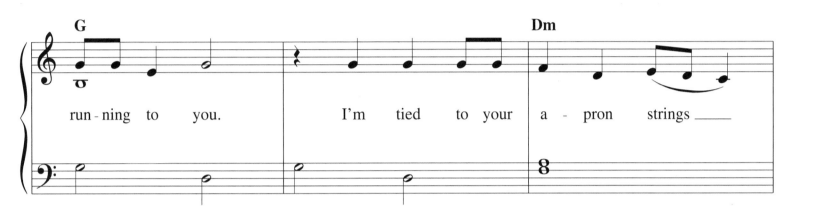

run - ning to you. I'm tied to your a - pron strings ____

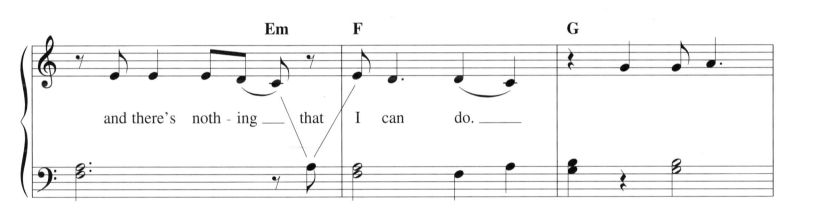

and there's noth - ing ____ that I can do. ____

G   **Dm**

Can't help my - self, __

Em   **F**   **G**   **D.S. al Coda**

no   I can't   help   my - self.

CODA

C

When   I   call   your   name,   girl,   it   starts   the   flame

burn - ing   in   my   heart,   tear - ing   it   all   a - part.   No

I HEAR A SYMPHONY

Words and Music by EDWARD HOLLAND,
LAMONT DOZIER and BRIAN HOLLAND

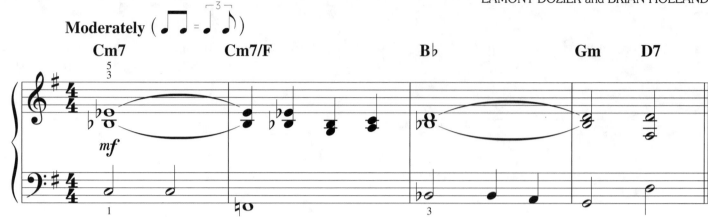

You've giv - en me a true love, and ev - 'ry day I

thank you love for a feel - ing that's so new,

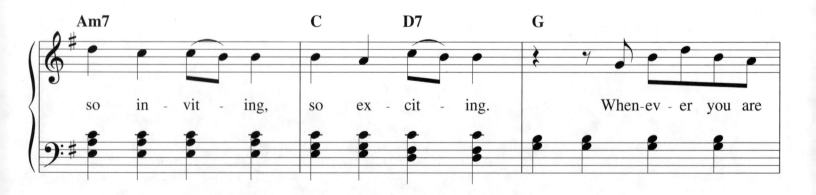

so in - vit - ing, so ex - cit - ing. When-ev - er you are

near, I hear a sym - pho - ny, a ten - der

mel - o - dy pull - ing me clos - er, closer

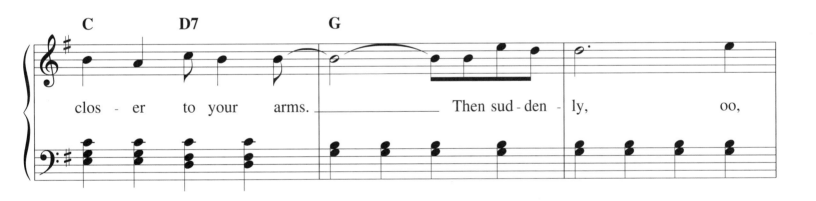

clos - er to your arms. _____ Then sud - den - ly, oo,

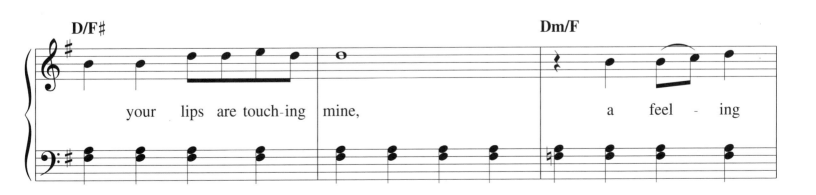

your lips are touch-ing mine, a feel - ing

so di - vine ____ 'til I leave _ the past be - hind. ____

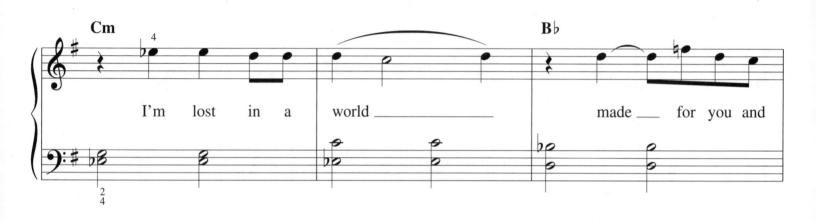

I'm lost in a world _____ made ___ for you and

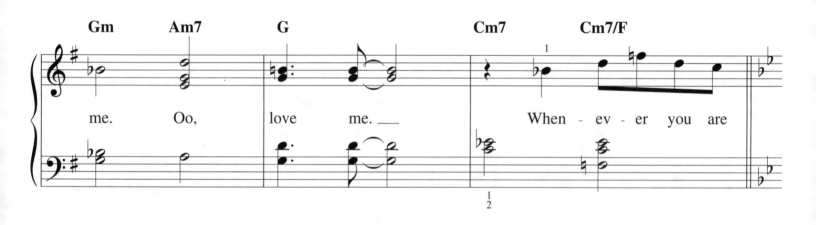

me. Oo, love me. ___ When - ev - er you are

near, ___ I hear a sym - pho - ny

play sweet and ten - der - ly _____ ev - 'ry

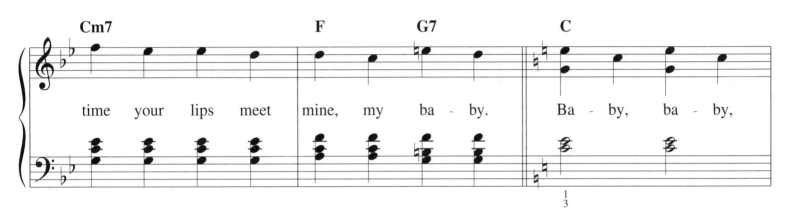

time your lips meet mine, my ba - by. Ba - by, ba - by,

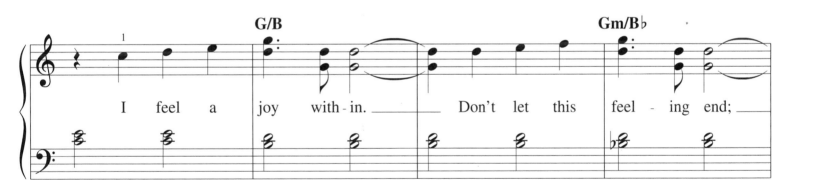

I feel a joy with - in. _____ Don't let this feel - ing end; _____

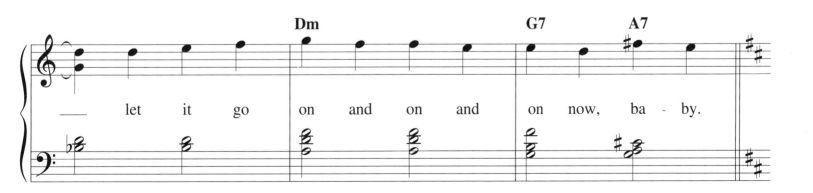

___ let it go on and on and on now, ba - by.

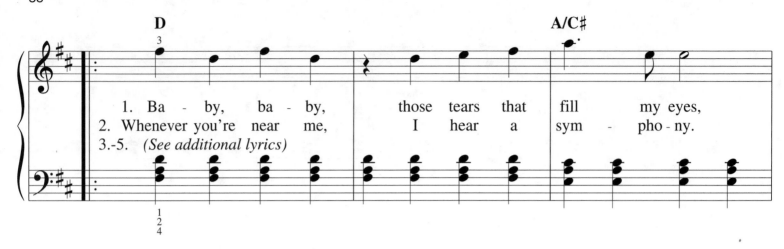

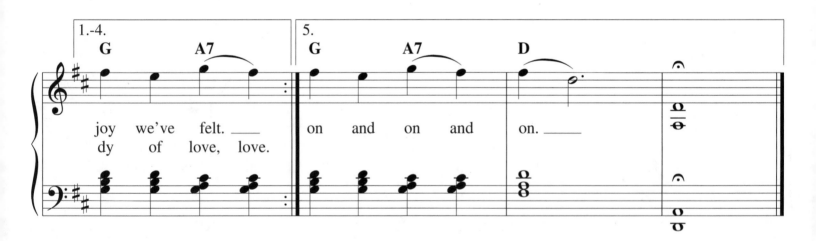

Additional Lyrics

3. Baby, baby, as you stand up holding me,
   Whispering how much you care,
   A thousand violins fill the air now.

4. Baby, baby, don't let this moment end,
   Keep standing close to me,
   Oo, so close to me.

5. Baby, baby, I hear a symphony,
   A tender melody. Ah, it goes
   On and on and on and on and on.

I HEARD IT THROUGH THE GRAPEVINE

Words and Music by NORMAN J. WHITFIELD
and BARRETT STRONG

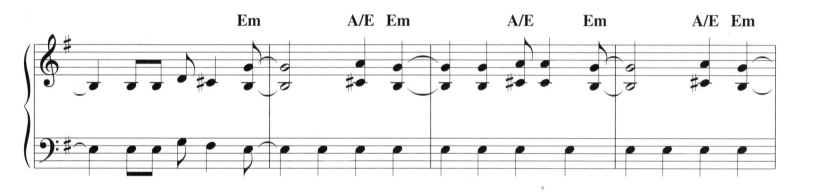

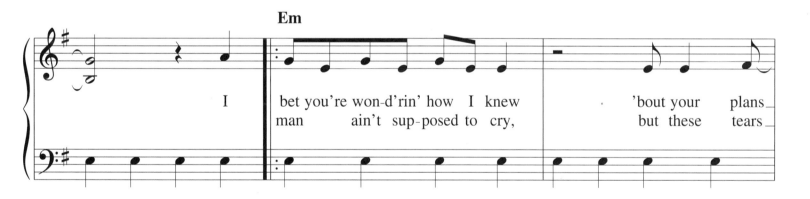

I bet you're won-d'rin' how I knew
man ain't sup-posed to cry,
'bout your plans
but these tears

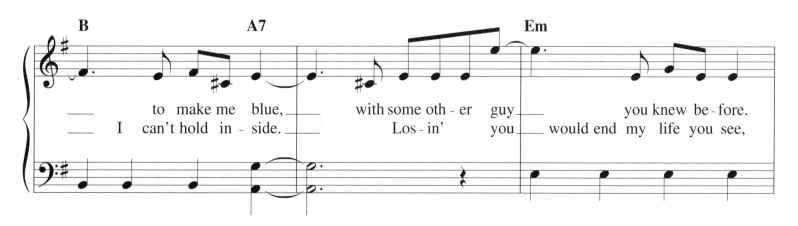

to make me blue, with some oth-er guy you knew be-fore.
I can't hold in-side. Los-in' you would end my life you see,

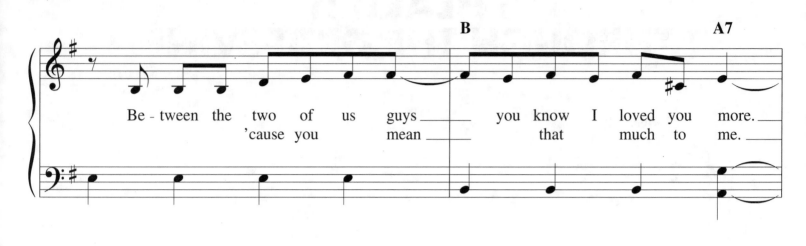

Be - tween the two of us guys _____ you know I loved you more. _____
'cause you mean _____ that much to me. _____

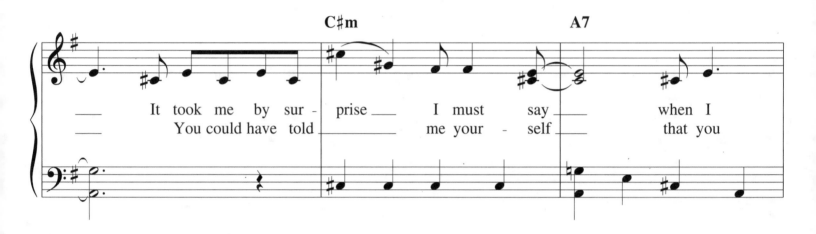

_____ It took me by sur - prise _____ I must say _____ when I
_____ You could have told _____ me your - self _____ that you

found out yes - ter - day. _____ Don't you know that I heard _____ it through the grape - vine,
loved _ some - one else. _____ In - stead _ I heard _____ it through the grape - vine,

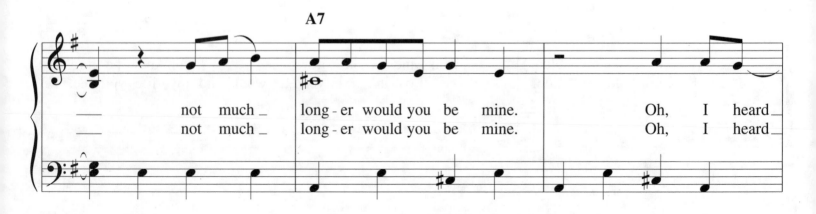

_____ not much _ long - er would you be mine. Oh, I heard
_____ not much _ long - er would you be mine. Oh, I heard _

it through the grape - vine.___ Oh, I'm just a - bout to lose ___ my
it through the grape - vine.___ And I'm just a - bout to lose ___ my

mind. Hon - ey, hon - ey, I heard it through the grape-vine, not much
mind.

long-er would you be mine, ba - by. I know a

I SECOND THAT EMOTION

Words and Music by WILLIAM "SMOKEY" ROBINSON
and ALFRED CLEVELAND

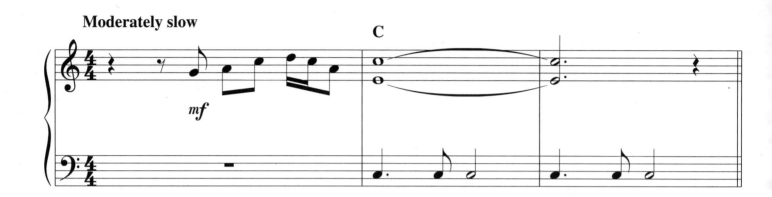

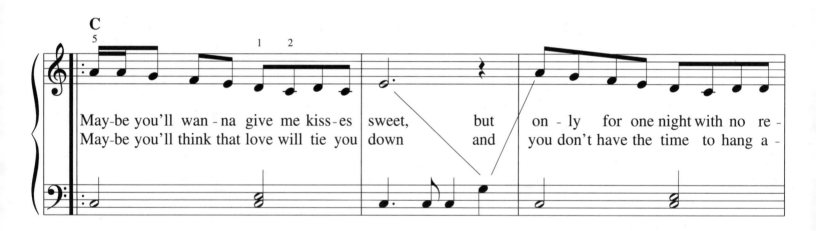

May-be you'll wan-na give me kiss-es sweet, but on - ly for one night with no re -
May-be you'll think that love will tie you down and you don't have the time to hang a -

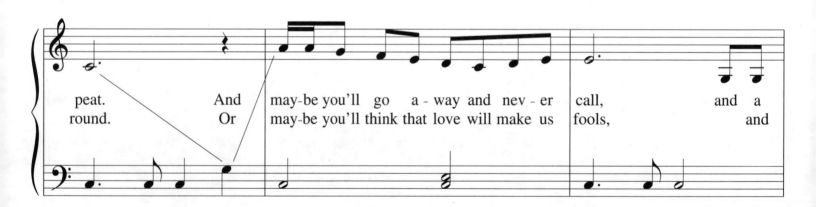

peat. And may-be you'll go a - way and nev - er call, and a
round. Or may-be you'll think that love will make us fools, and

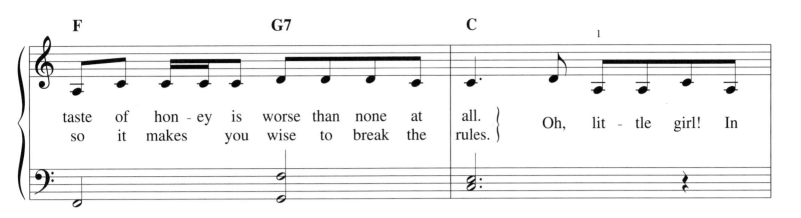

taste of hon - ey is worse than none at all.
so it makes you wise to break the rules. Oh, lit - tle girl! In

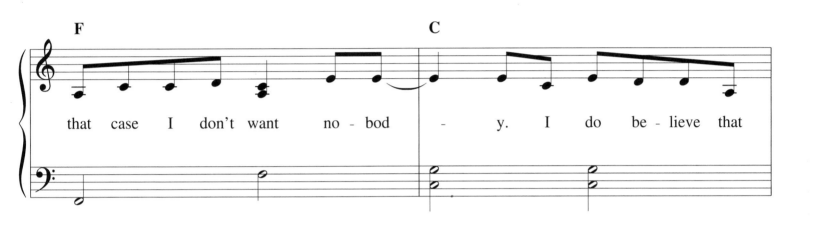

that case I don't want no - bod - y. I do be - lieve that

that would on - ly break __ my heart. ___ Oh, but

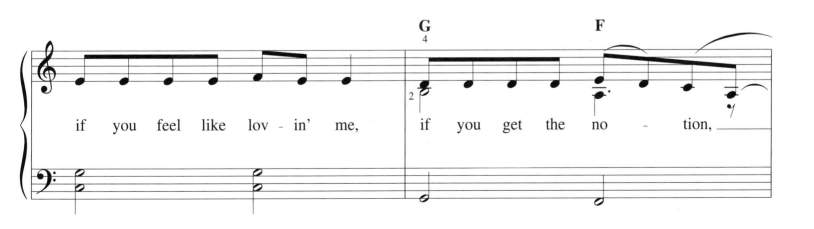

if you feel like lov - in' me, if you get the no - tion, ___

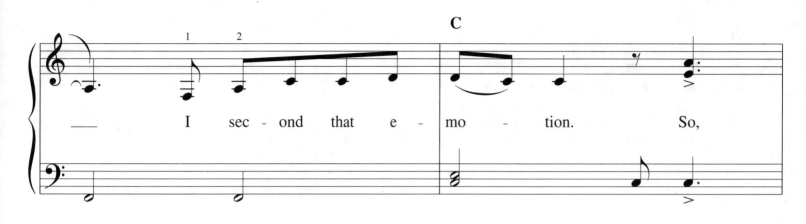

I sec - ond that e - mo - tion. So,

if you feel like giv - ing me a life - time of de - vo - tion,

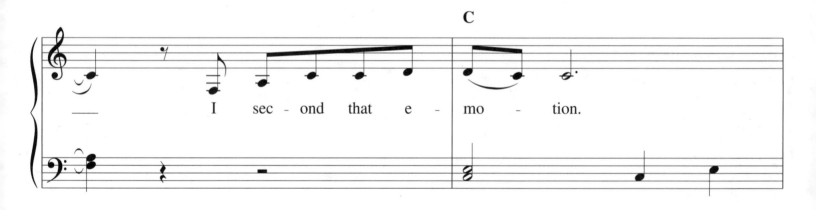

I sec - ond that e - mo - tion.

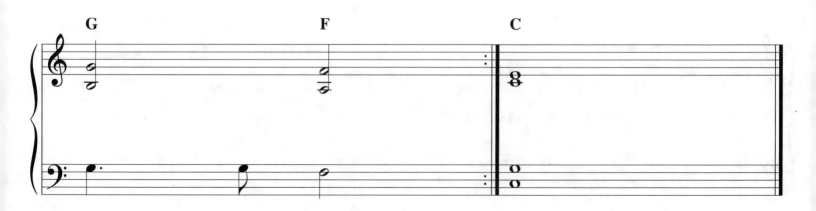

IT'S THE SAME OLD SONG

Words and Music by EDWARD HOLLAND,
LAMONT DOZIER and BRIAN HOLLAND

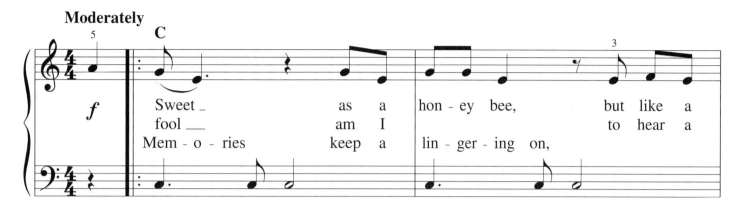

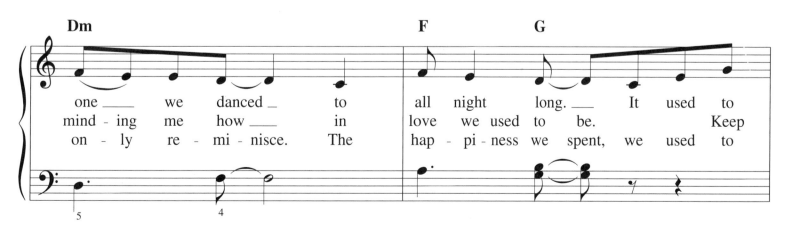

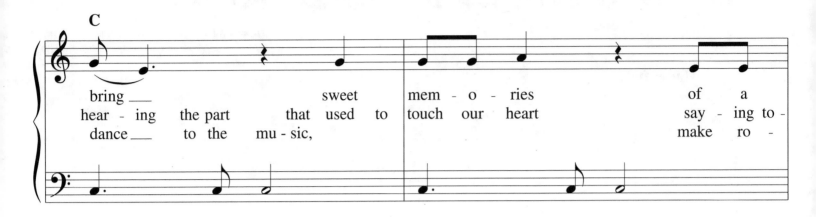

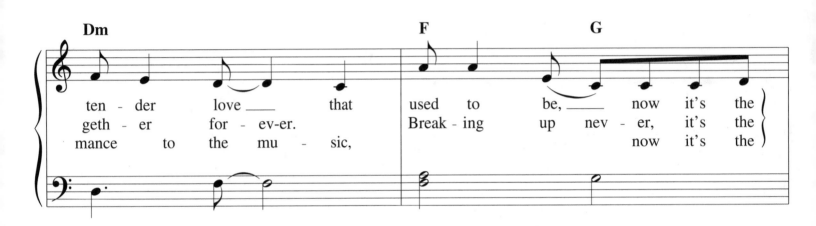

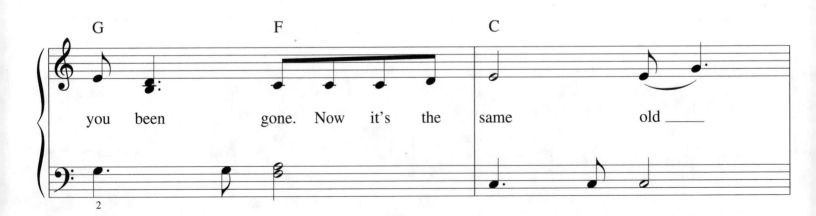

song   but with a   dif‑f'rent   mean – ing   since ‑ a

you been   gone.   Sen ‑ ti ‑ men ‑ tal

I'LL BE THERE

Words and Music by BERRY GORDY, HAL DAVIS,
WILLIE HUTCH and BOB WEST

Moderately

You and I must make a pact;
Let me fill your heart with joy and laugh-ter;

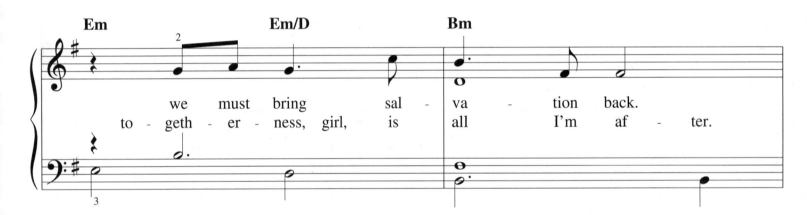

we must bring sal - va - tion back.
to - geth - er - ness, girl, is all I'm af - ter.

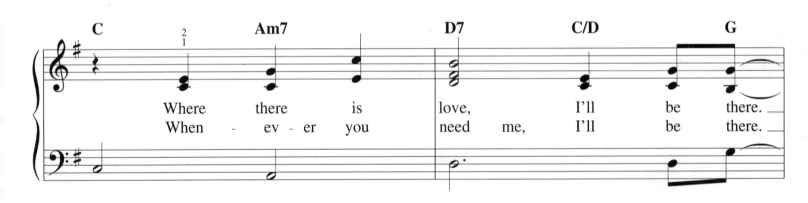

Where there is love, I'll be there.
When - ev - er you need me, I'll be there.

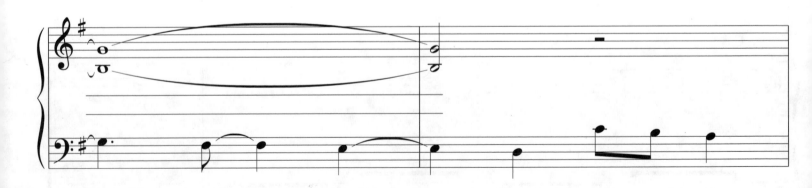

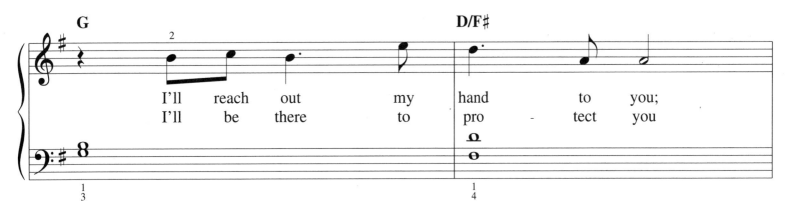

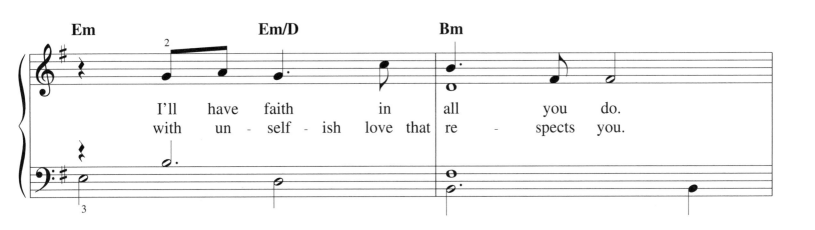

To Coda ⊕

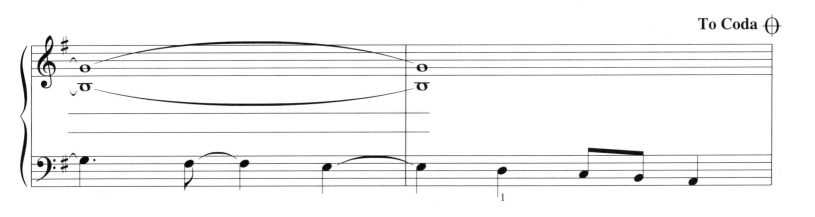

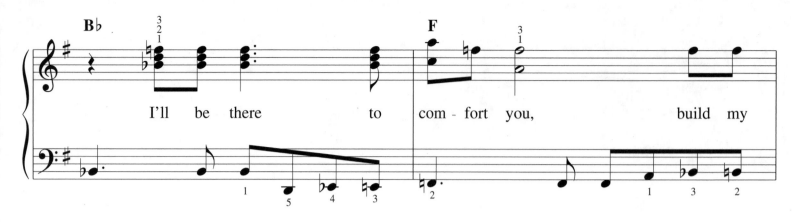

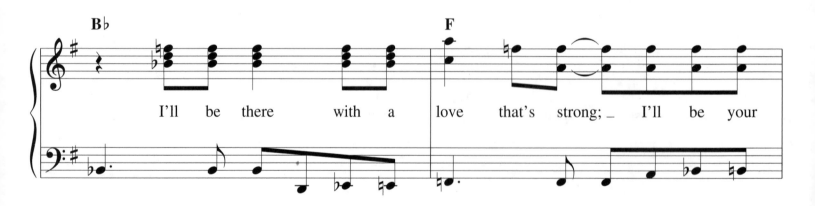

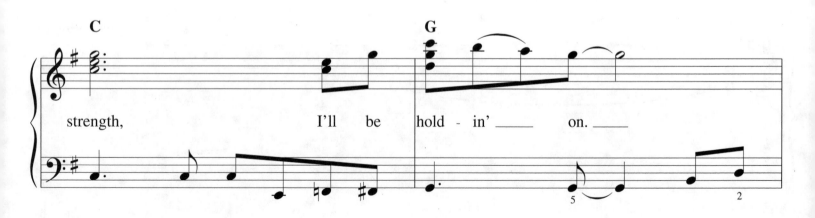

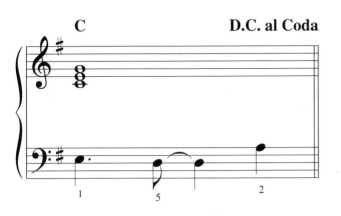

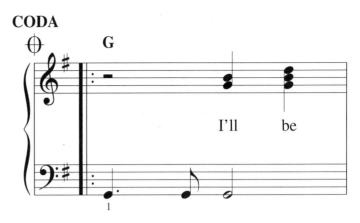

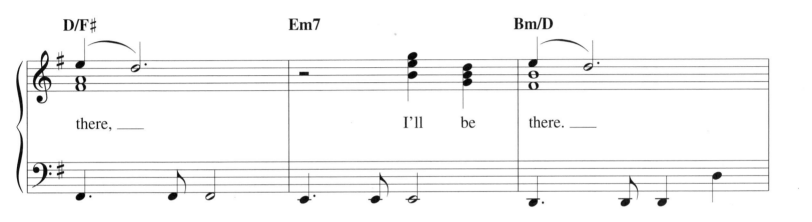

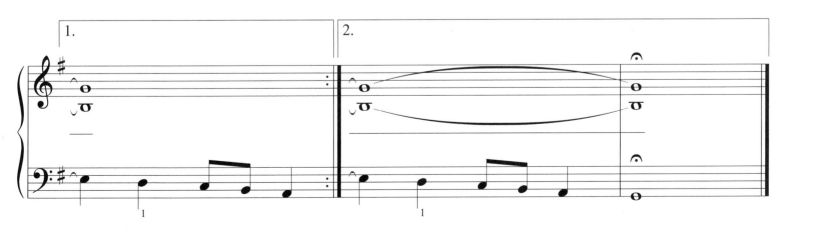

IF I WERE YOUR WOMAN

Words and Music by LAVERNE WARE,
PAM SAWYER and CLAY McMURRAY

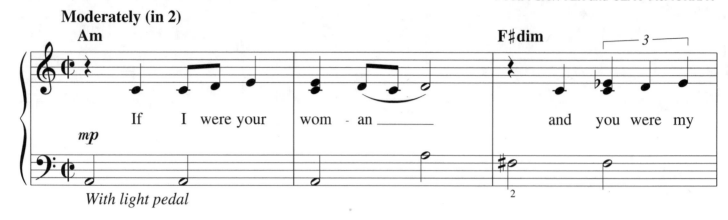

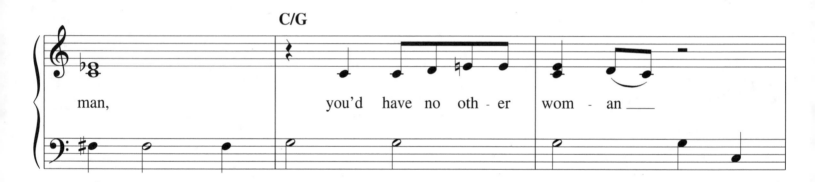

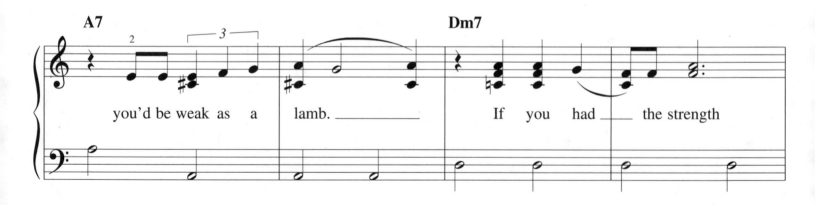

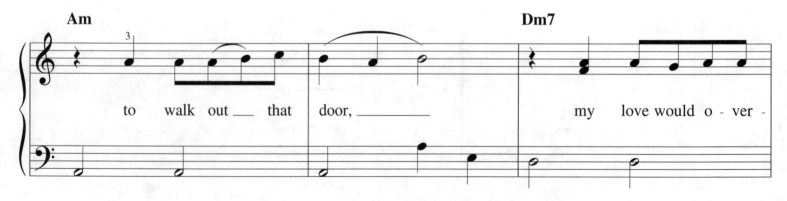

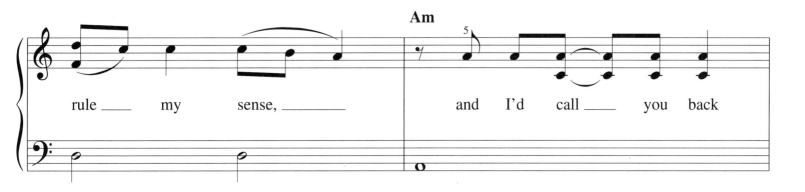

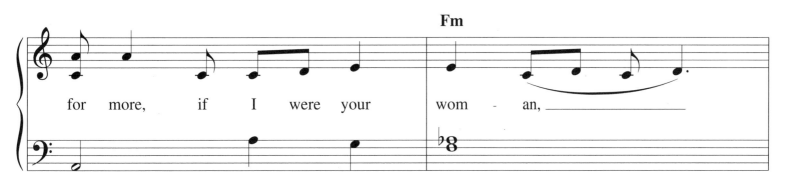

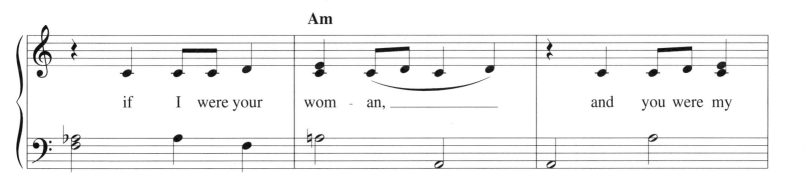

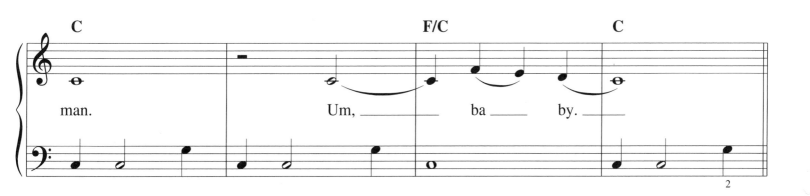

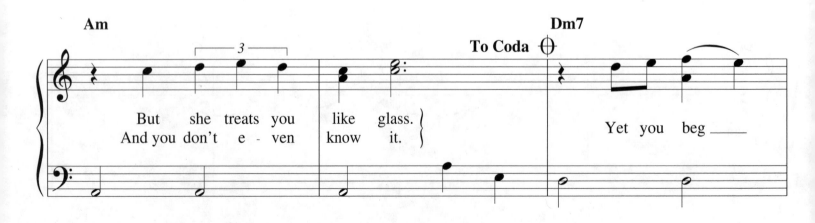

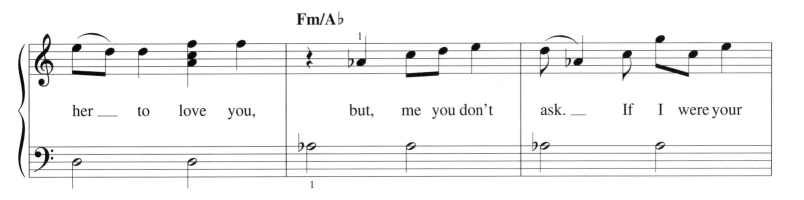

her ___ to love you, but, me you don't ask. ___ If I were your

wom - an, _____ if I were your wom - an, _____

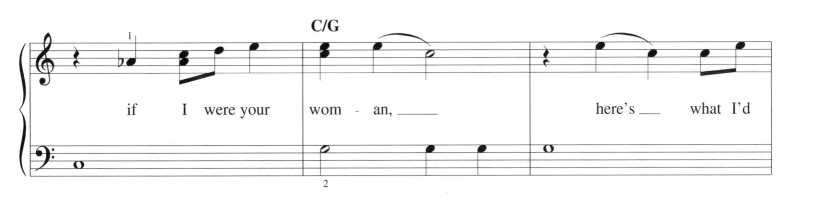

if I were your wom - an, _____ here's ___ what I'd

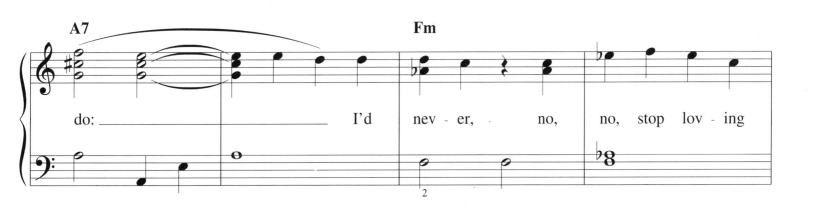

do: _____ I'd nev - er, no, no, stop lov - ing

you. _____   Yeah, _____

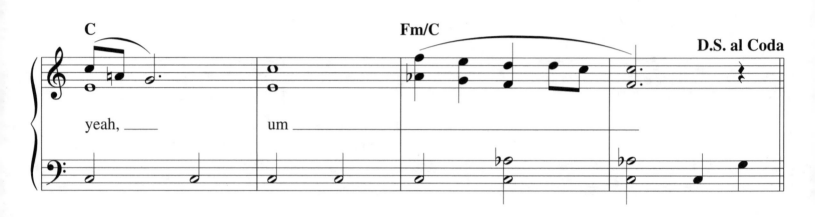

yeah, _____   um _____   D.S. al Coda

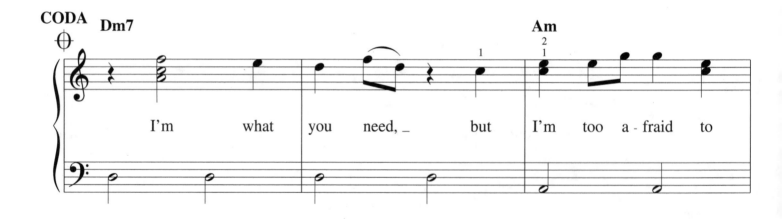

I'm   what   you   need, _   but   I'm   too   a - fraid   to

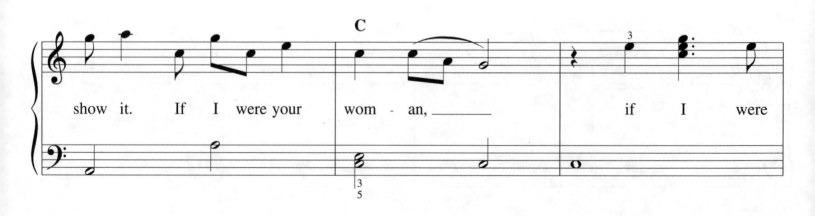

show it.   If   I   were   your   wom - an, _____   if   I   were

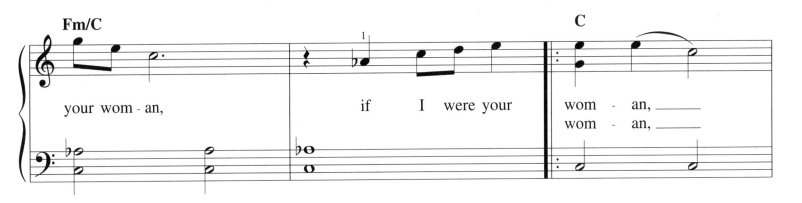

your wom - an,   if   I   were your   wom - an, _____
                                                             wom - an, _____

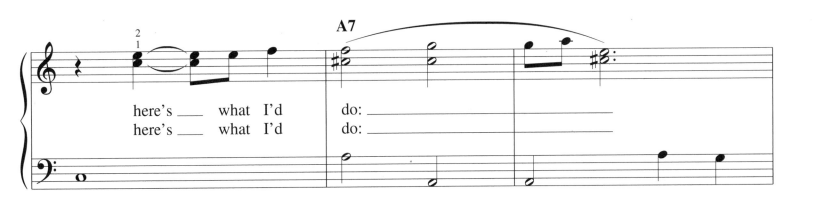

here's ___ what I'd   do: _____
here's ___ what I'd   do: _____

Nev - er, no, ___ no,   no, stop lov - ing ___ you, ___
Nev - er, nev - er   stop lov - ing you if   I were your

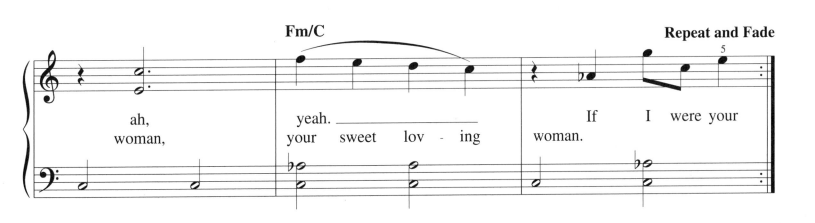

ah,   yeah. _____   If   I   were your
woman,   your sweet lov - ing   woman.

THE LOVE YOU SAVE

Words and Music by BERRY GORDY,
ALPHONSO MIZELL, FREDDIE PERREN
and DENNIS LUSSIER

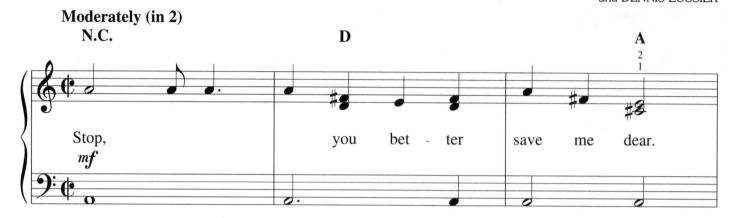

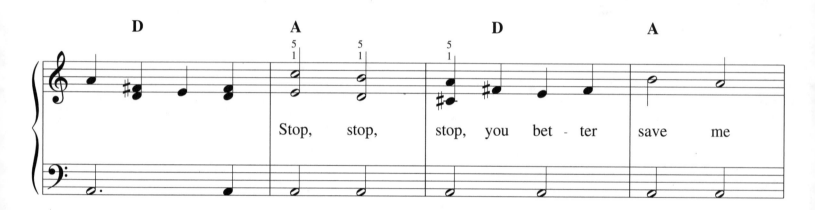

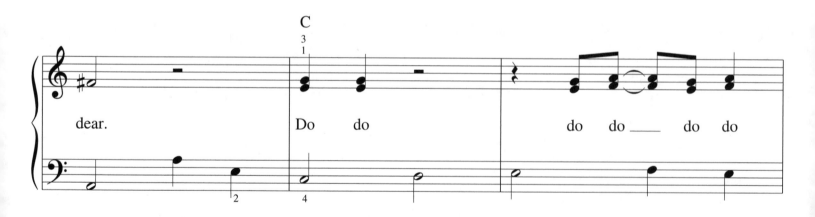

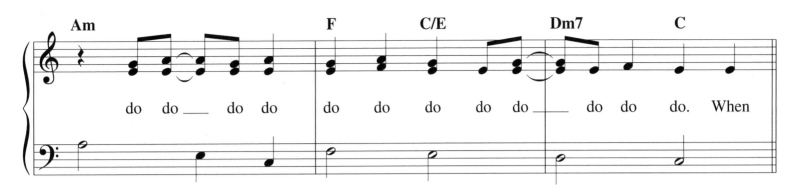

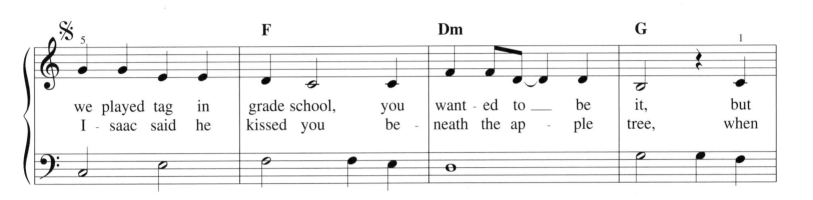

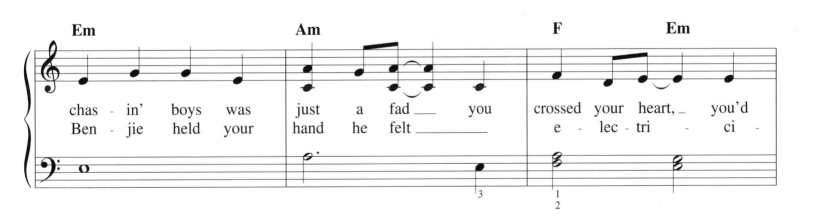

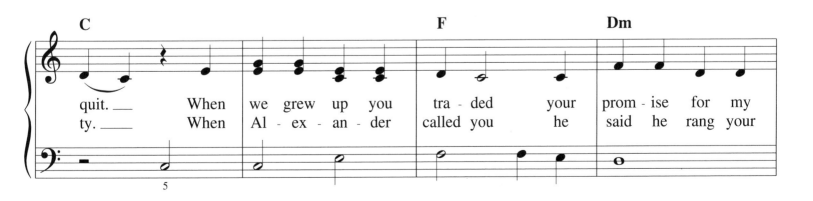

60

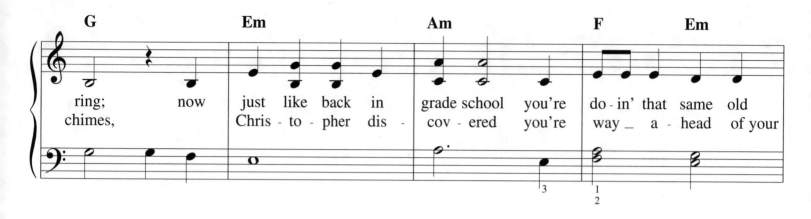

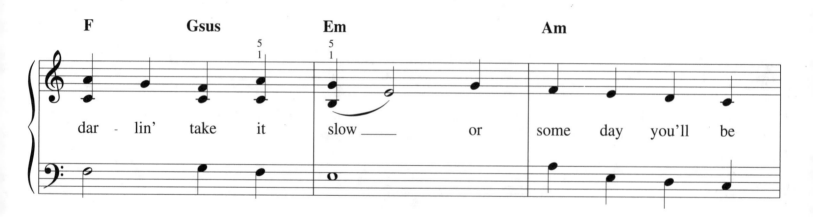

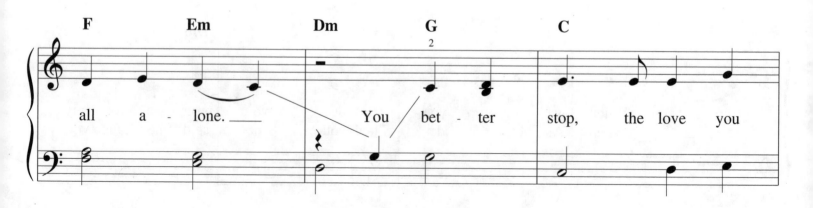

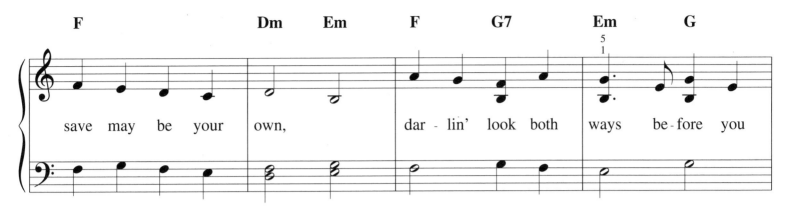

save may be your own, dar - lin' look both ways be - fore you

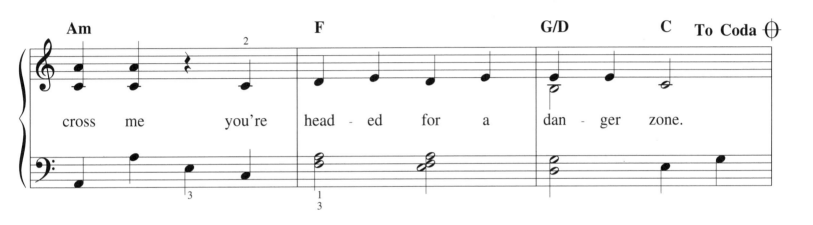

cross me you're head - ed for a dan - ger zone.

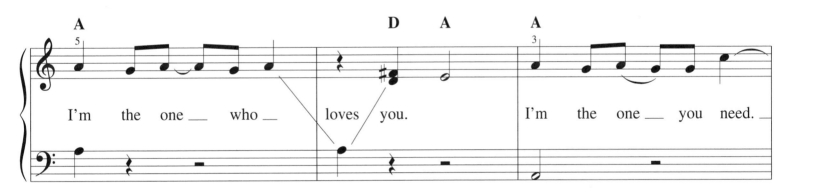

I'm the one __ who __ loves you. I'm the one __ you need. __

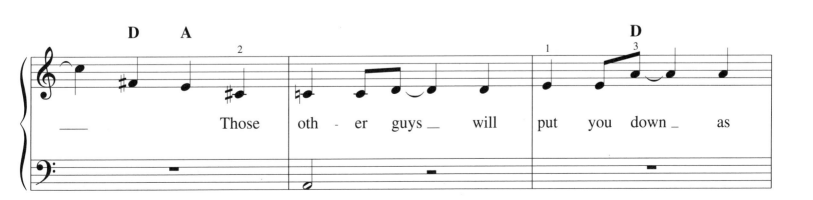

__ Those oth - er guys __ will put you down __ as

soon as they suc - ceed. They - 'll ru - in your rep - u - ta -

tion. They - 'll la - bel you ___ a flirt. ___ The

D.S. al Coda

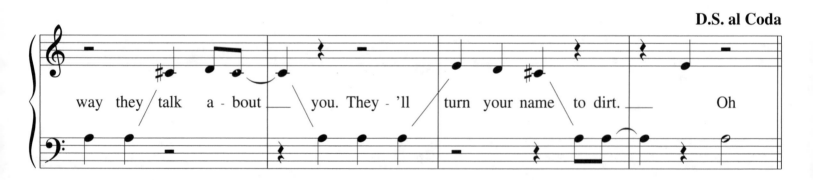

way they talk a - bout ___ you. They - 'll turn your name to dirt. ___ Oh

CODA

Play 4 times

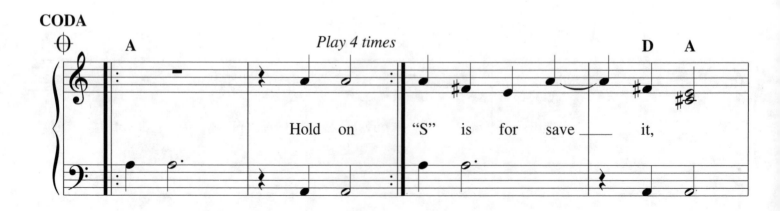

Hold on "S" is for save ___ it,

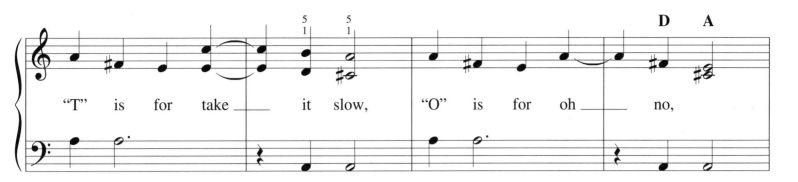

"T" is for take ___ it slow, "O" is for oh ___ no,

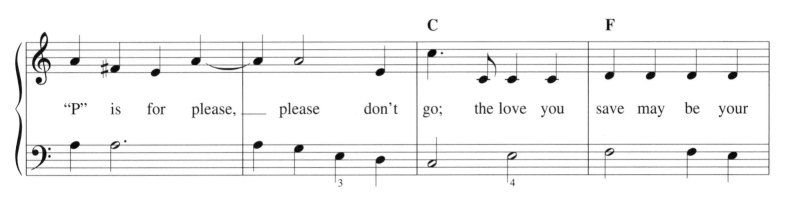

"P" is for please, ___ please don't go; the love you save may be your

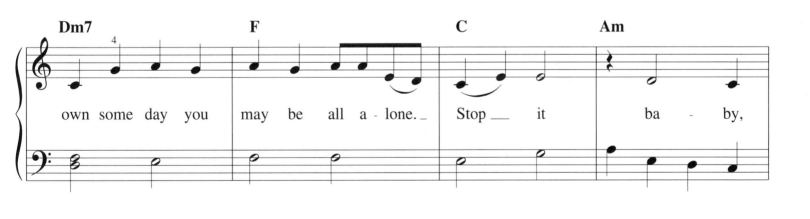

own some day you may be all a - lone. ___ Stop ___ it ba - by,

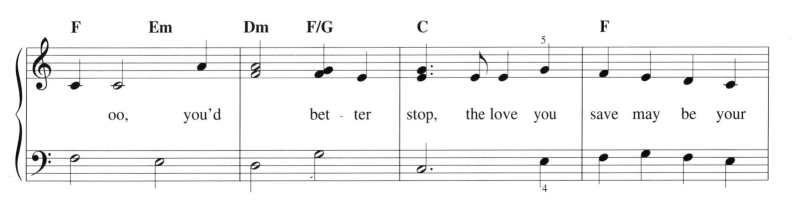

oo, you'd bet - ter stop, the love you save may be your

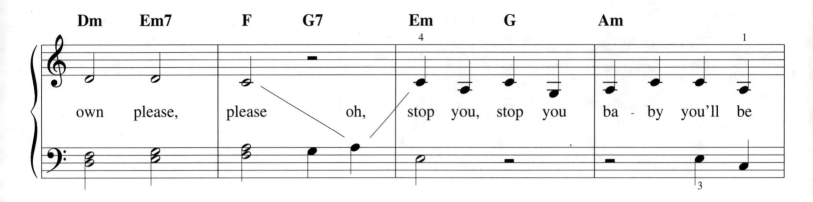

own please, please oh, stop you, stop you ba - by you'll be

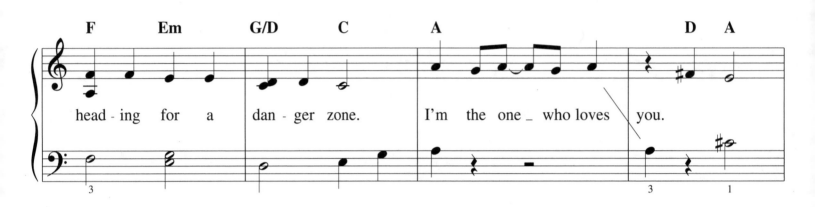

head - ing for a dan - ger zone. I'm the one _ who loves you.

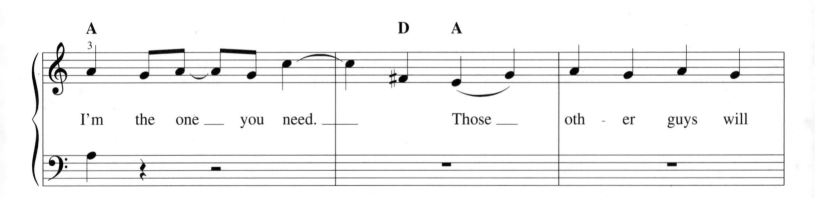

I'm the one _ you need. _ Those _ oth - er guys will

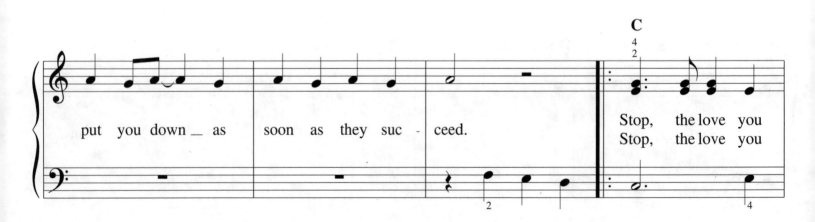

put you down _ as soon as they suc - ceed. Stop, the love you
                     Stop, the love you

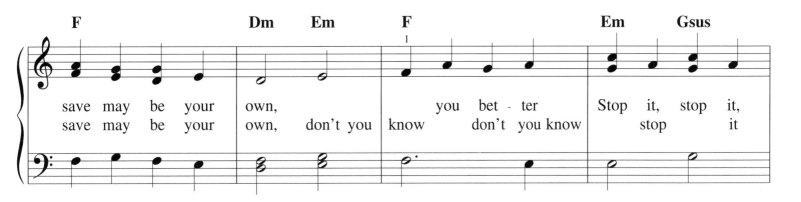

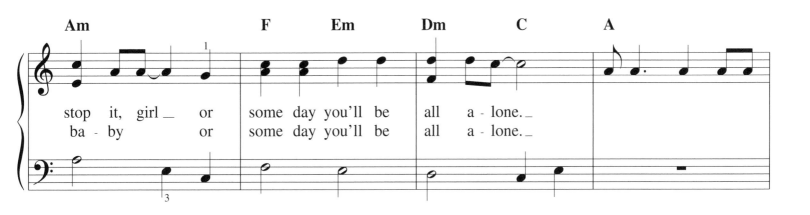

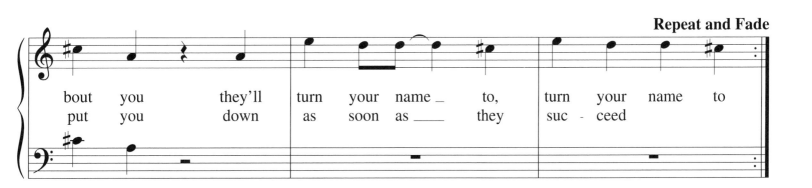

MAYBE TOMORROW

Words and Music by BERRY GORDY,
ALPHONSO J. MIZELL, FREDERICK J. PERREN
and DENNIS LUSSIER

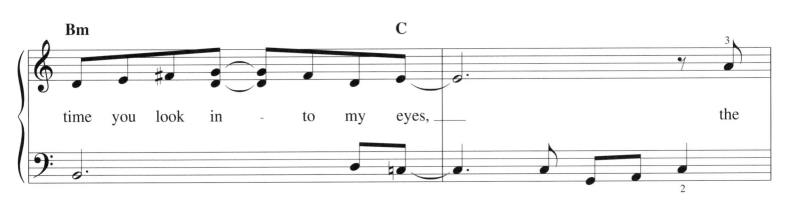

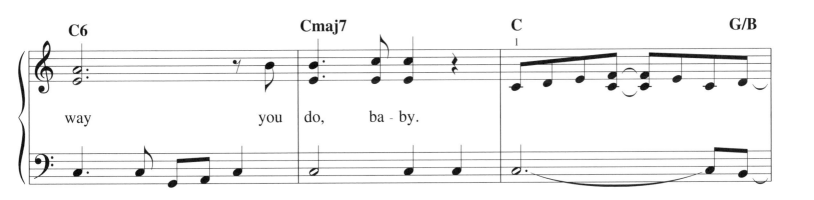

beau - ti - ful bird, ___ you have flown ___ a - way.   I

Inst. solo ad lib.

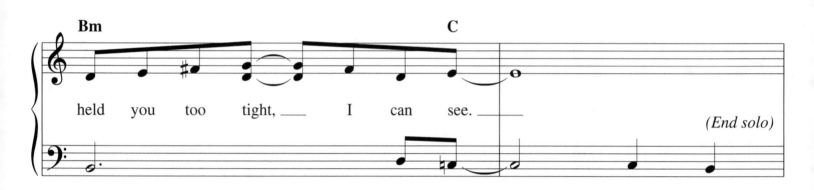

held   you   too   tight, ___   I   can   see. ___

(End solo)

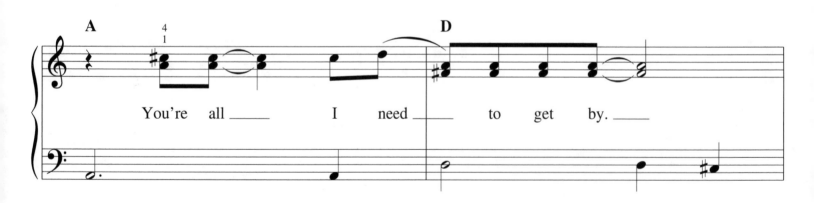

You're all ___   I   need ___   to   get   by. ___

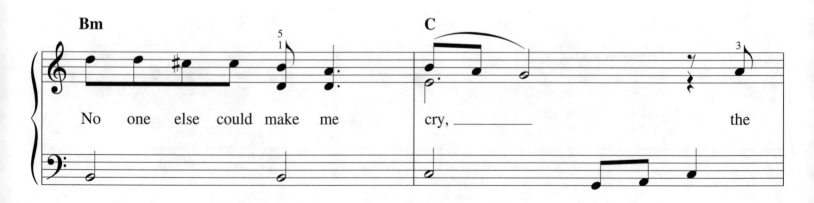

No   one   else   could   make   me   cry, ___   the

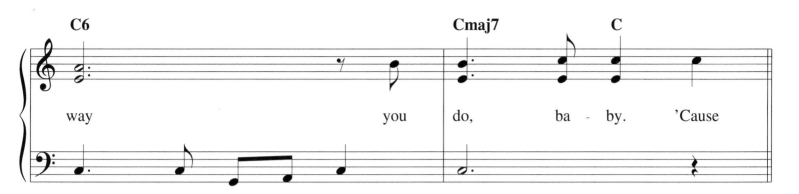

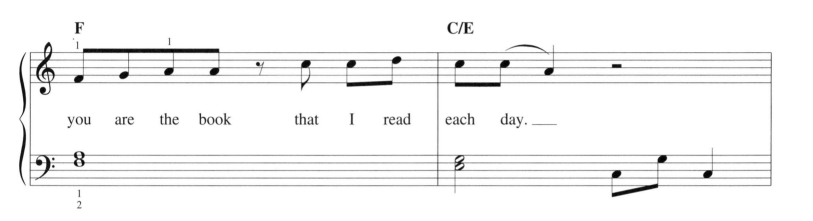

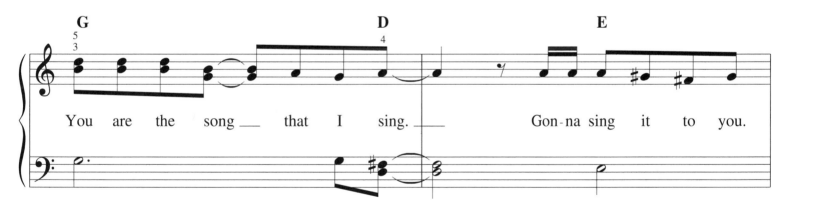

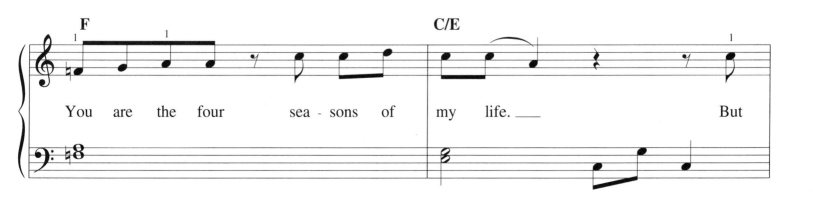

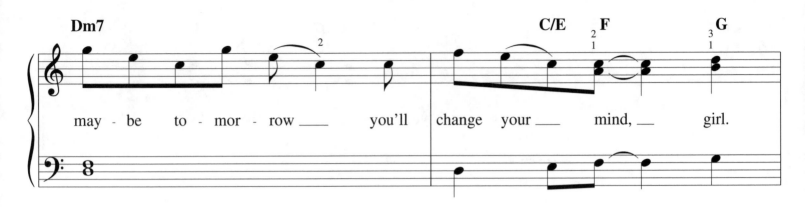

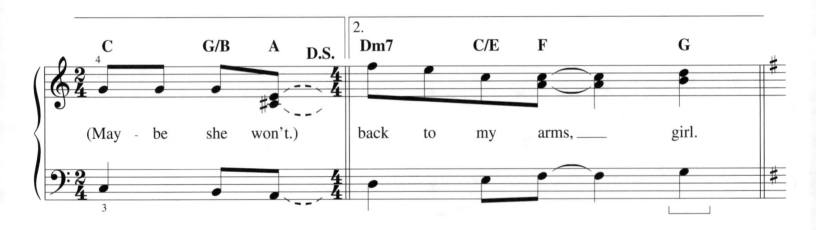

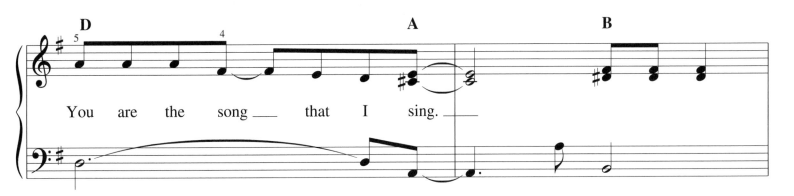

You are the song ___ that I sing. ___

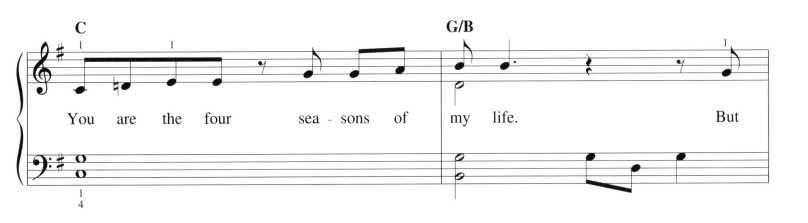

You are the four sea - sons of my life. But

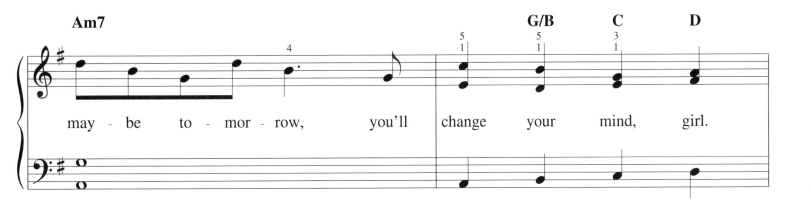

may - be to - mor - row, you'll change your mind, girl.

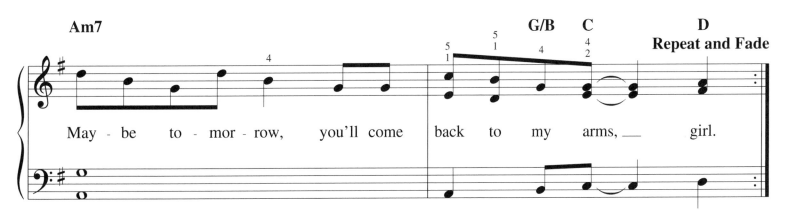

May - be to - mor - row, you'll come back to my arms, ___ girl.

MERCY, MERCY ME
(THE ECOLOGY)

Words and Music by
MARVIN GAYE

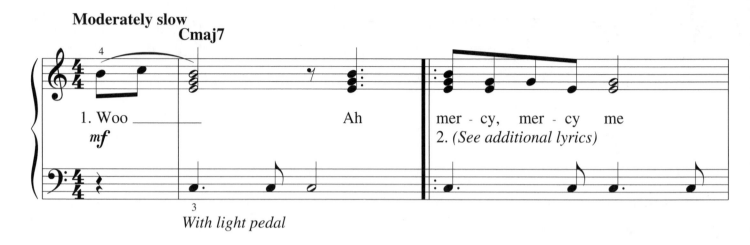

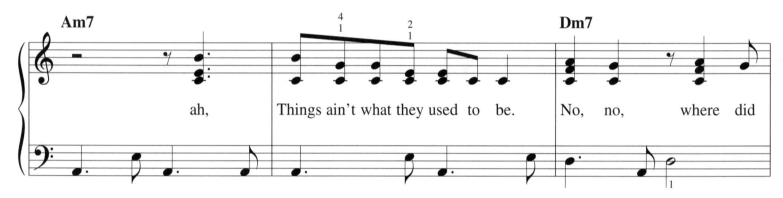

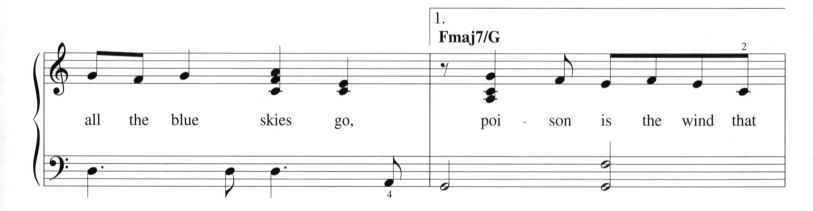

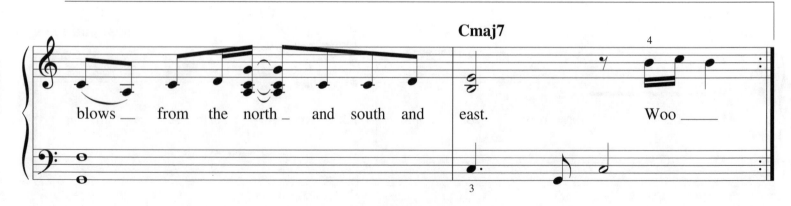

2.
Fmaj7/G   **Cmaj7**

up - on our seas fish full of mer - cu - ry, ah. _____ Oh

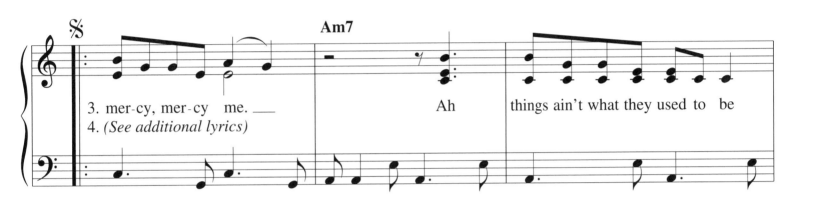

Am7

3. mer-cy, mer-cy me. ____ Ah things ain't what they used to be
4. *(See additional lyrics)*

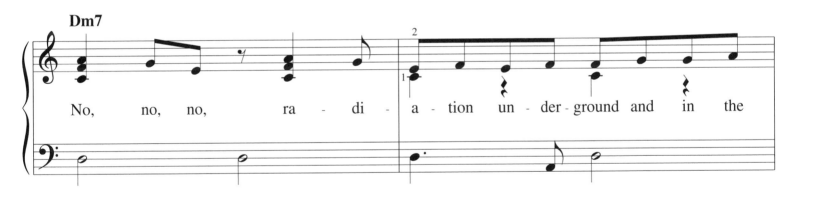

Dm7

No, no, no, ra - di - a - tion un - der - ground and in the

Fmaj7/G   1.   **C**   **Cmaj7**

sky; an - i - mals and birds who live near - by are dy - ing. Oh,

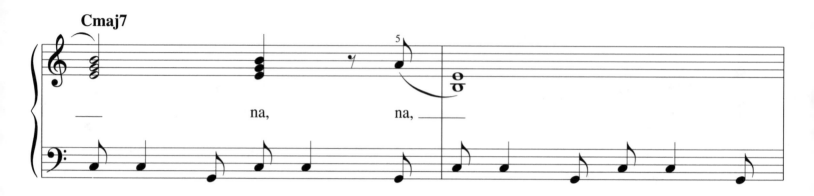

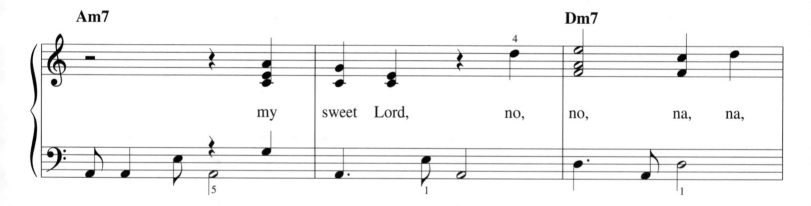

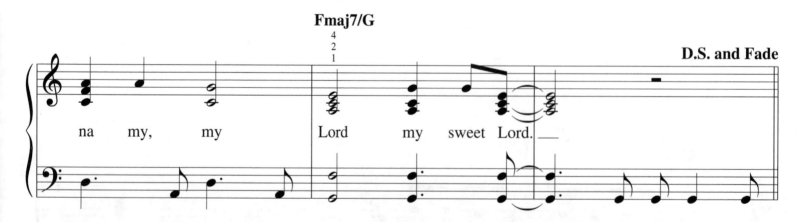

Additional Lyrics

2. Mercy, mercy me
   Ah things ain't what they used to be, no, no
   Oil wasted on the ocean and upon
   Our seas fish full of mercury, ah.

4. Mercy, mercy me
   Ah things ain't what they used to be
   What about this over-crowded land
   How much more abuse from man can she stand?

MY CHERIE AMOUR

Words and Music by STEVIE WONDER,
SYLVIA MOY and HENRY COSBY

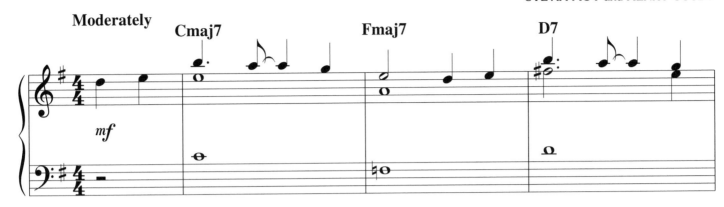

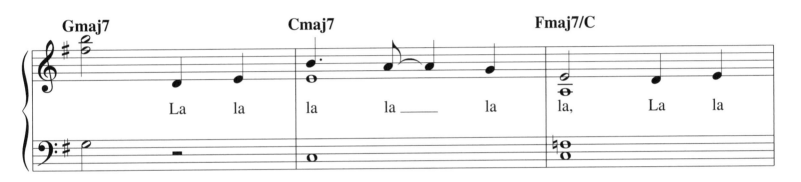

La la la la _____ la la, La la

la la _____ la la. My Che - rie A - mour, _____
ca - fé _____ or
some _____ day _____ you'll

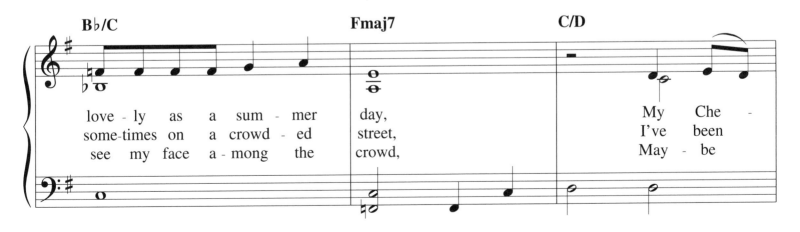

love - ly as a sum - mer day, My Che -
some - times on a crowd - ed street, I've been
see my face a - mong the crowd, May - be

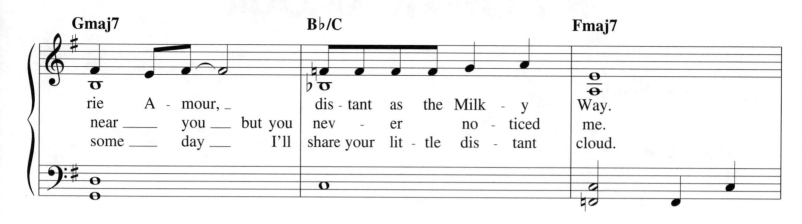

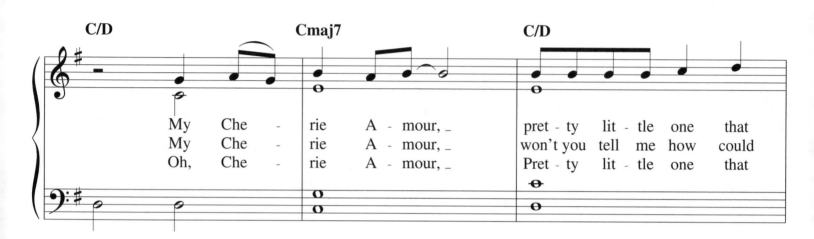

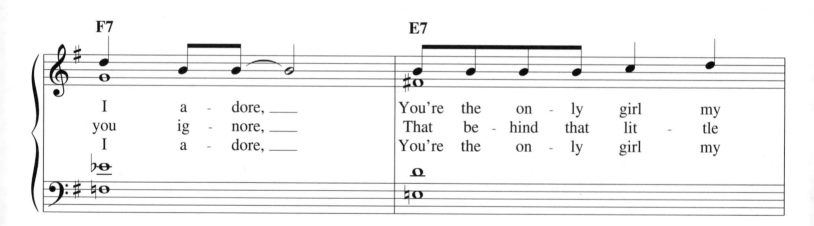

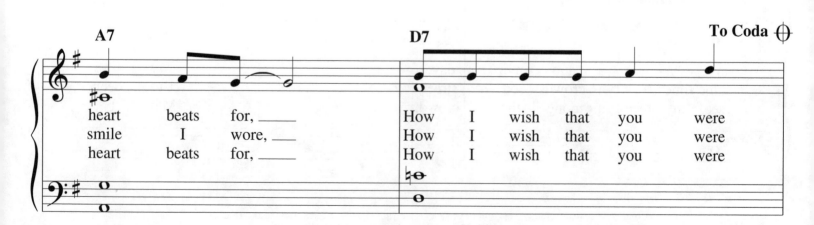

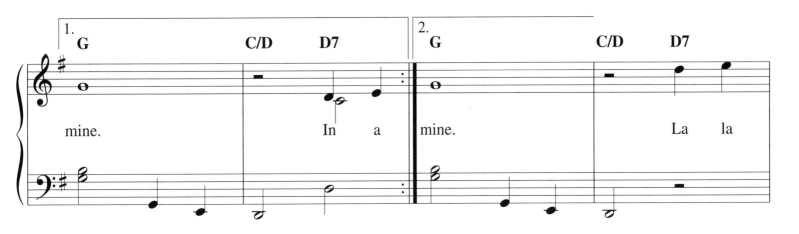

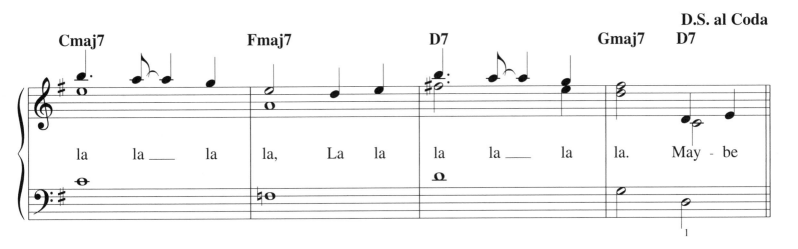

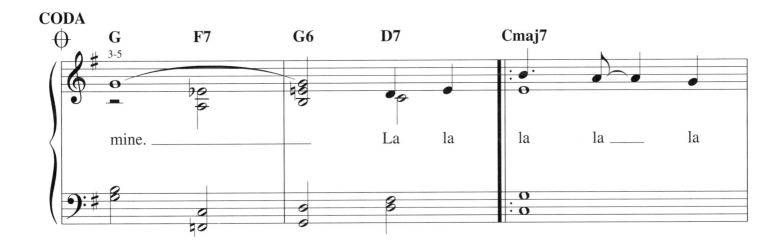

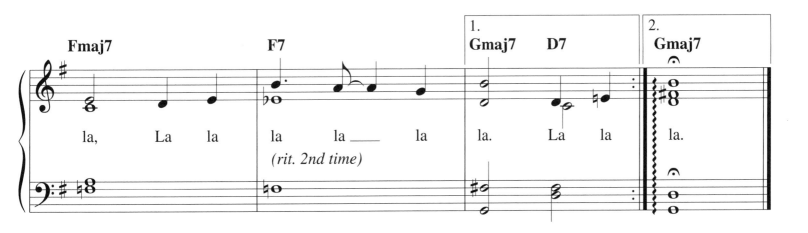

MY GIRL

Words and Music by WILLIAM "SMOKEY" ROBINSON
and RONALD WHITE

I've got a sweet-er song _____ than the birds in the

trees.

CODA

Well,

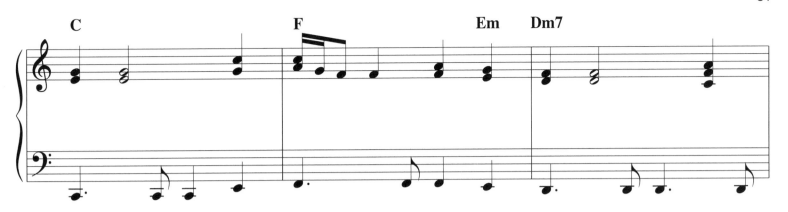

I don't

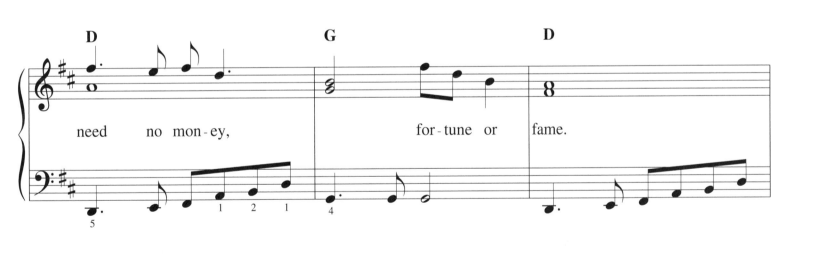

need   no mon-ey,   for-tune or   fame.

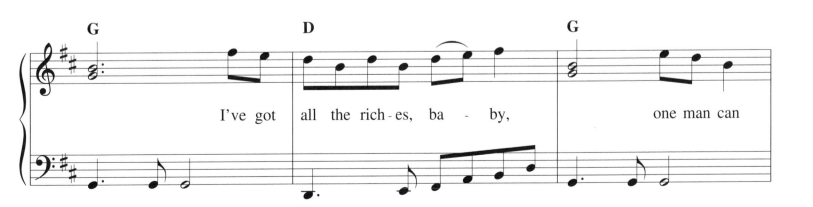

I've got   all the rich-es, ba - by,   one man can

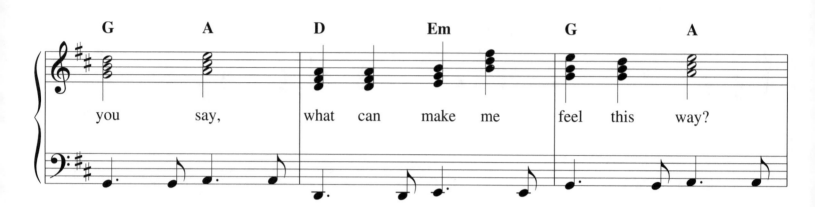

cloud - y day with my girl. _____ I've e - ven got the month of May with

my girl. _____ Talk-ing 'bout, _ talk-ing 'bout, _ talk-ing 'bout _

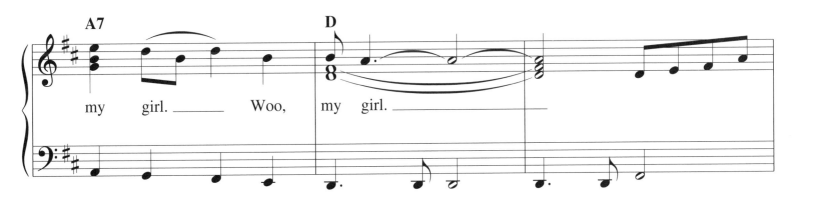

my girl. _____ Woo, my girl. _____

That's all I can talk a - bout is my girl. _____

MY GUY

Words and Music by
WILLIAM "SMOKEY" ROBINSON

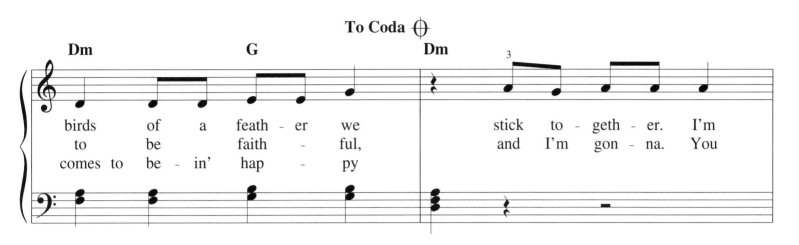

To Coda

Dm   G   Dm

birds   of   a   feath - er   we   stick   to - geth - er.   I'm
to   be   faith - ful,   and   I'm   gon - na.   You
comes   to   be - in'   hap - py

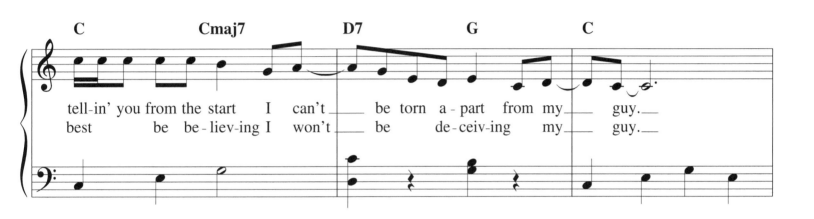

C   Cmaj7   D7   G   C

tell - in' you from the start   I   can't ___ be torn a - part   from my ___ guy. ___
best   be be - liev - ing I   won't ___ be de - ceiv - ing   my ___ guy. ___

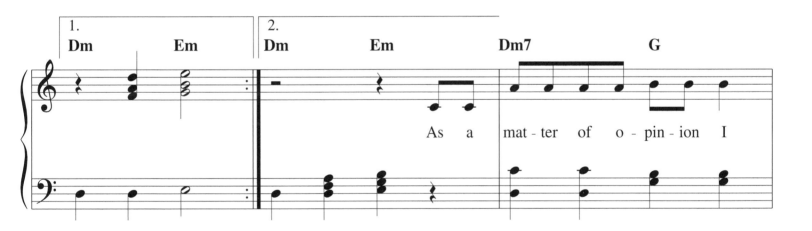

1.
Dm   Em

2.
Dm   Em   Dm7   G

As   a   mat - ter   of   o - pin - ion   I

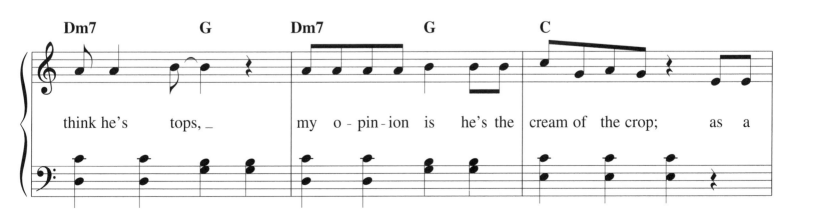

Dm7   G   Dm7   G   C

think he's   tops, _   my   o - pin - ion   is   he's the   cream   of   the crop;   as   a

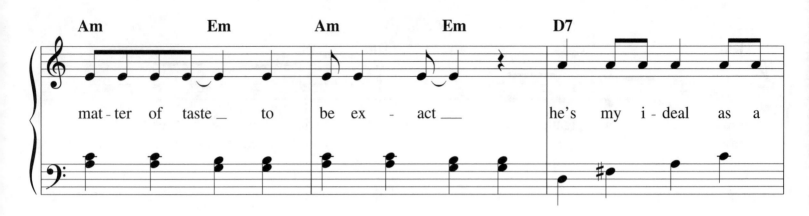

mat - ter of taste __ to be ex - act __ he's my i - deal as a

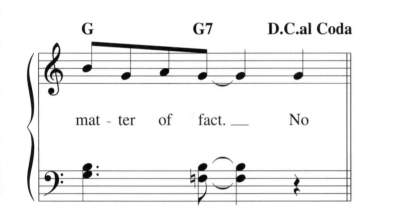

mat - ter of fact. __ No

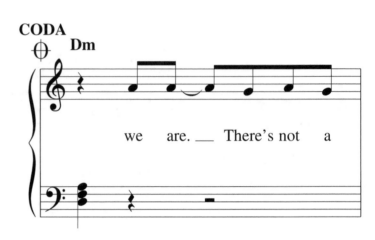

CODA

we are. __ There's not a

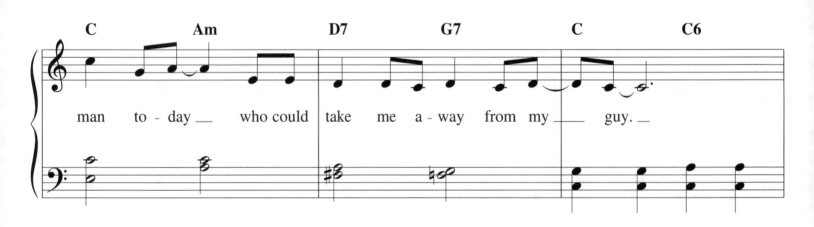

man to - day __ who could take me a - way from my __ guy. __

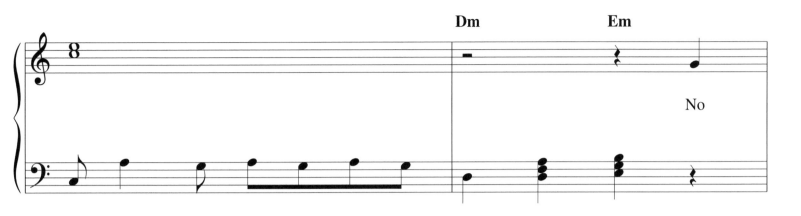

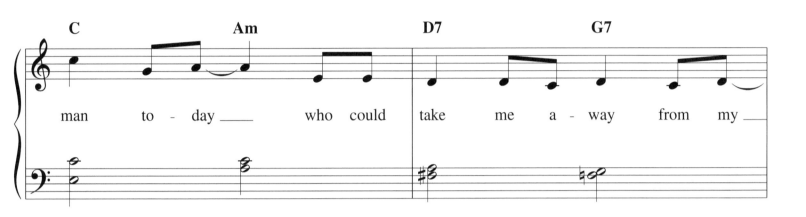

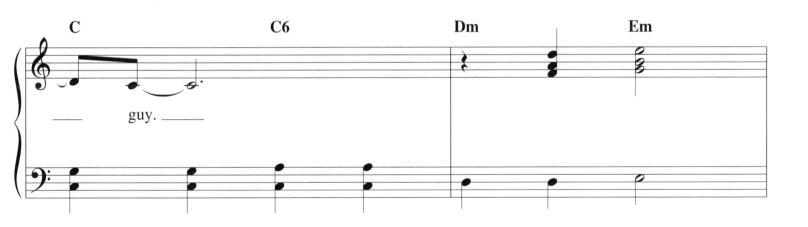

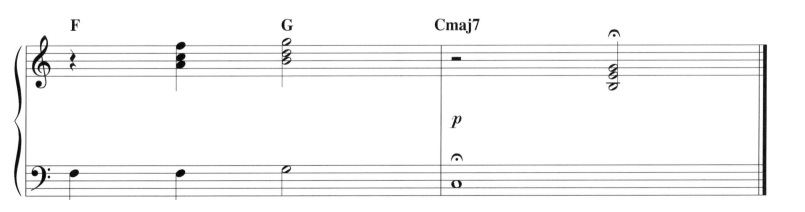

NEVER CAN SAY GOODBYE

Words and Music by
CLIFTON DAVIS

Moderately

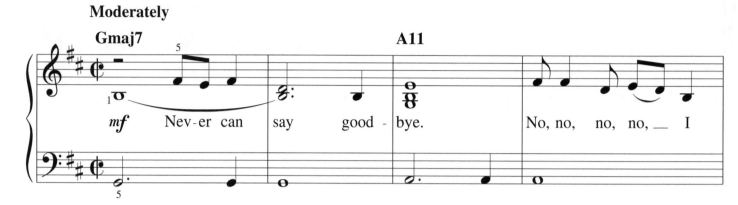

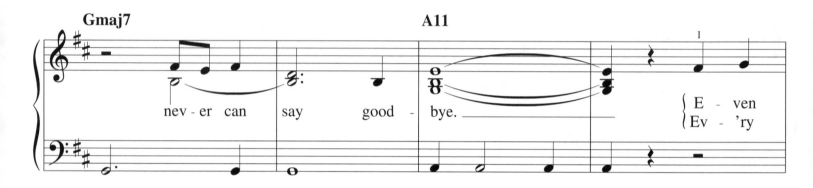

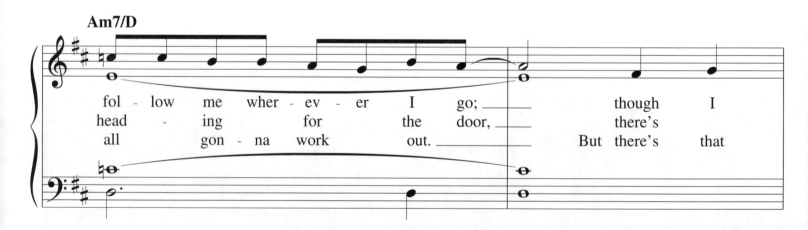

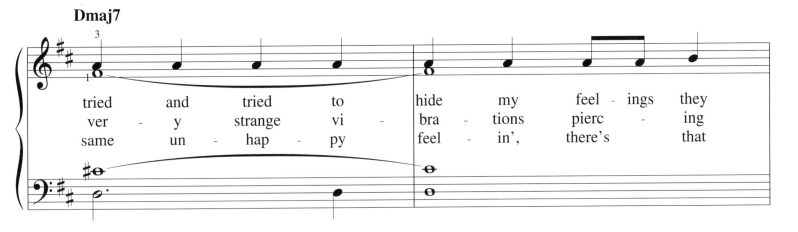

Dmaj7

tried and tried to hide my feel - ings they
ver - y strange vi - bra - tions pierc - ing
same un - hap - py feel - in', there's that

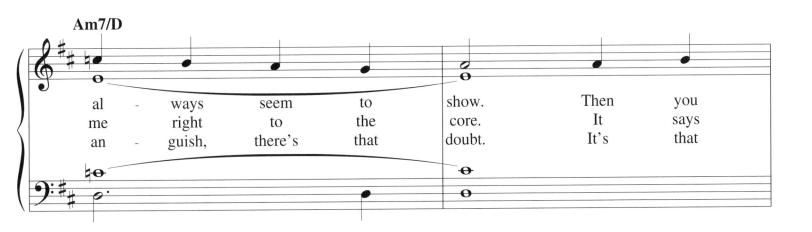

Am7/D

al - ways seem to show. Then you
me right to the core. It says
an - guish, there's the that doubt. It's that

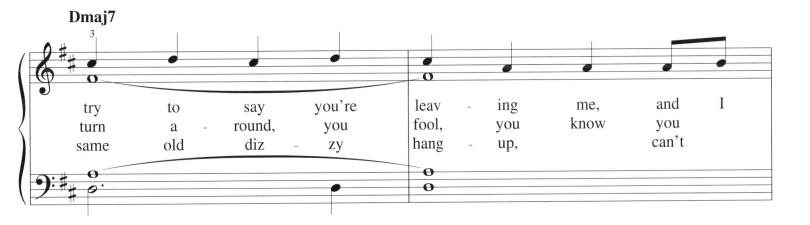

Dmaj7

try to say you're leav - ing me, and I
turn a - round, you fool, you know you
same old diz - zy hang - up, can't

Am7/D

al - ways have to say no. Tell me
love her more and more.
do with you or with - out.

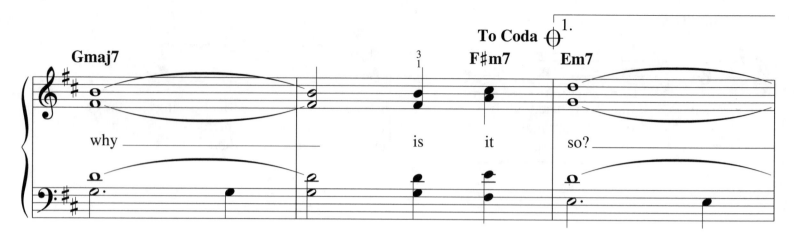

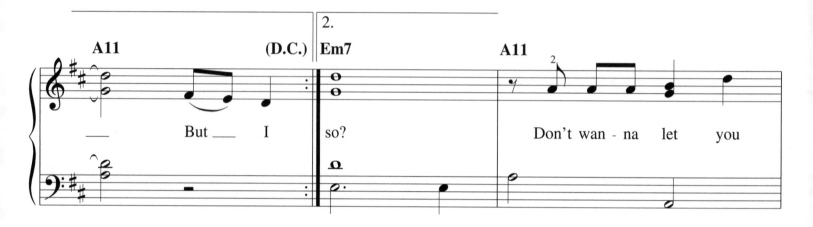

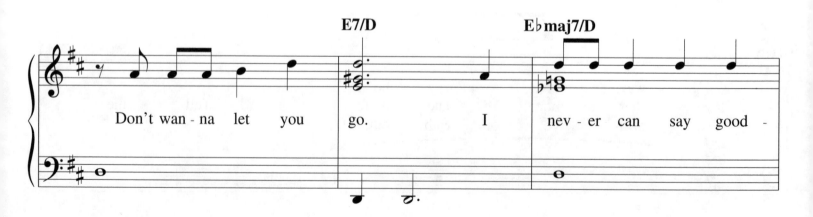

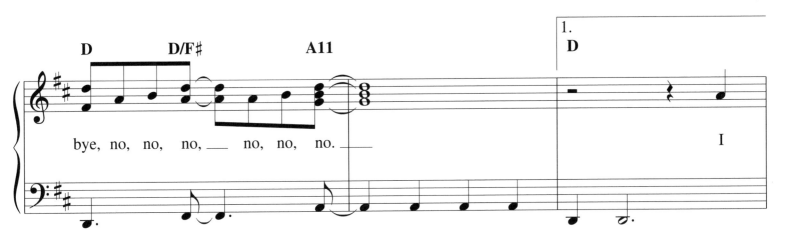

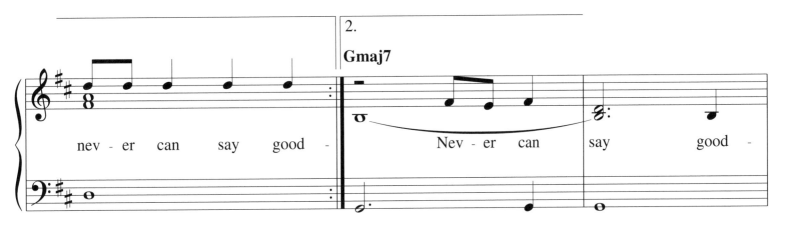

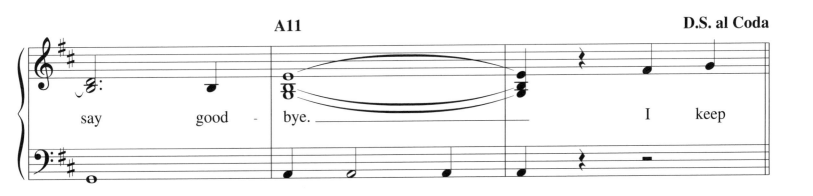

CODA

so? Don't wan-na let you go. I

nev-er can say good-bye, girl. Don't wan-na let you

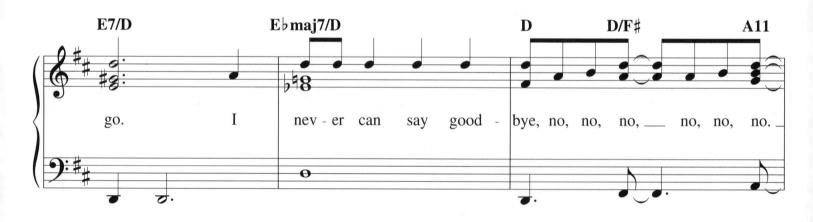

go. I nev-er can say good-bye, no, no, no, ___ no, no, no.

I nev-er can say good-

REACH OUT AND TOUCH
(Somebody's Hand)

Words and Music by NICKOLAS ASHFORD
and VALERIE SIMPSON

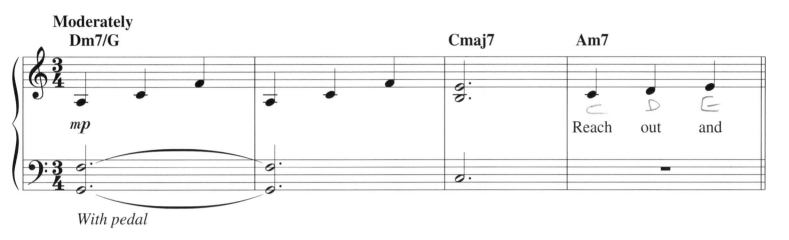

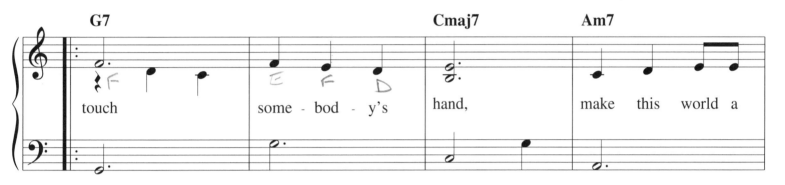

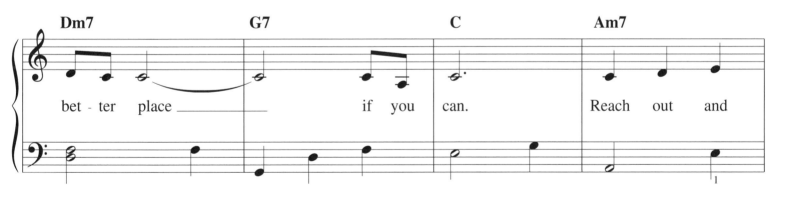

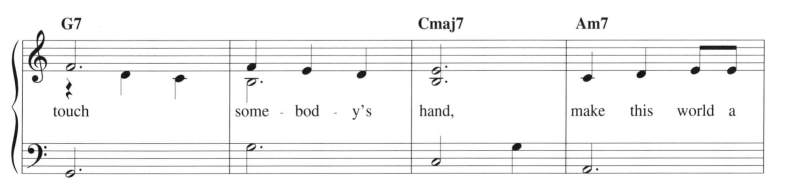

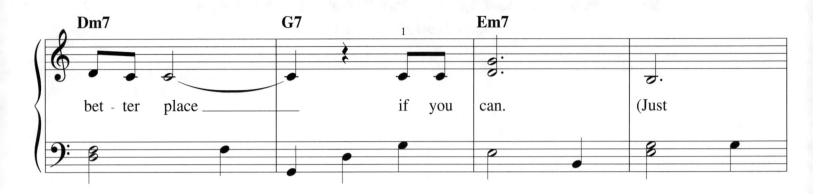

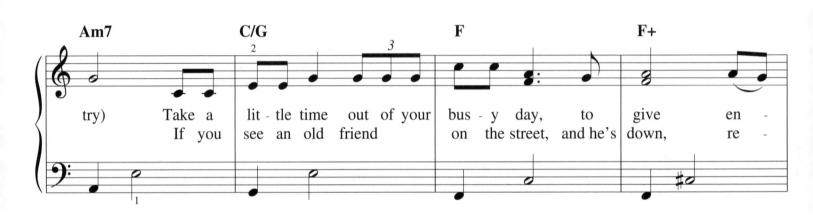

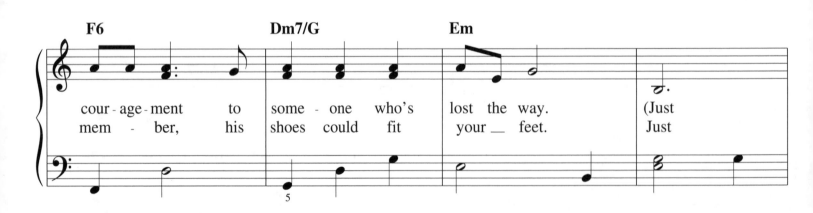

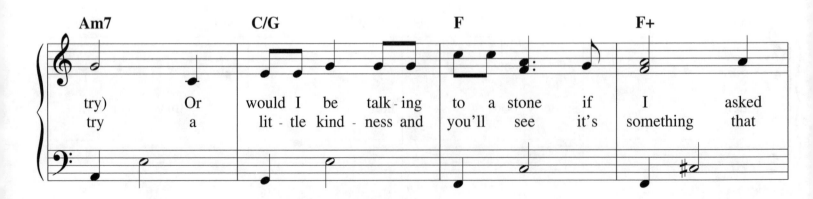

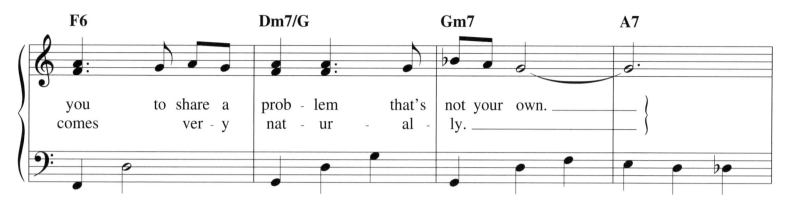

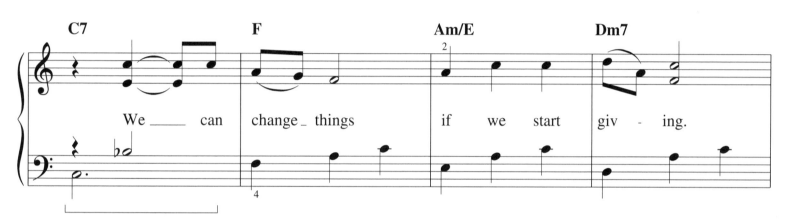

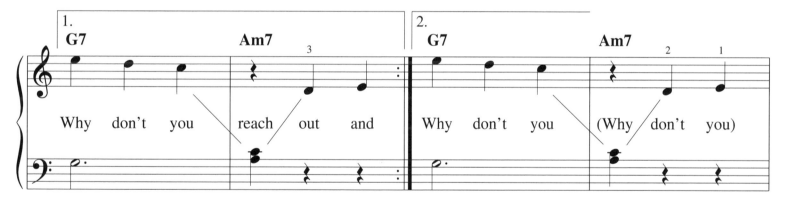

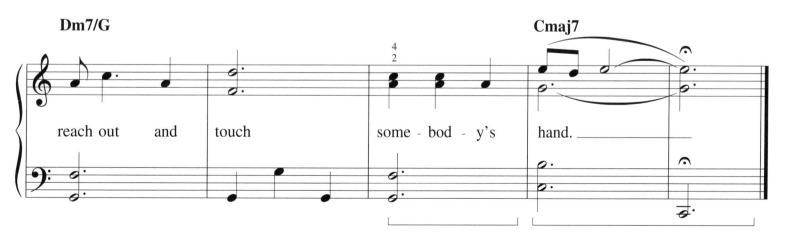

OOO BABY BABY

Words and Music by WILLIAM "SMOKEY" ROBINSON
and WARREN MOORE

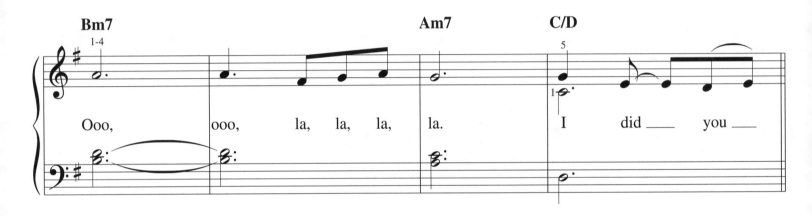

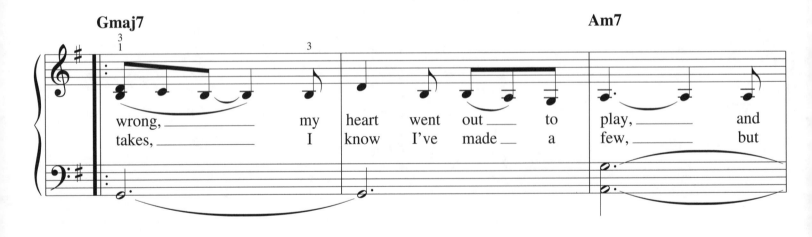

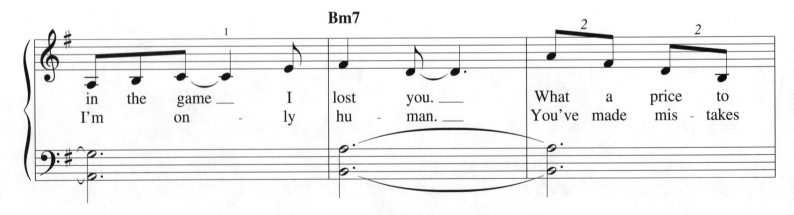

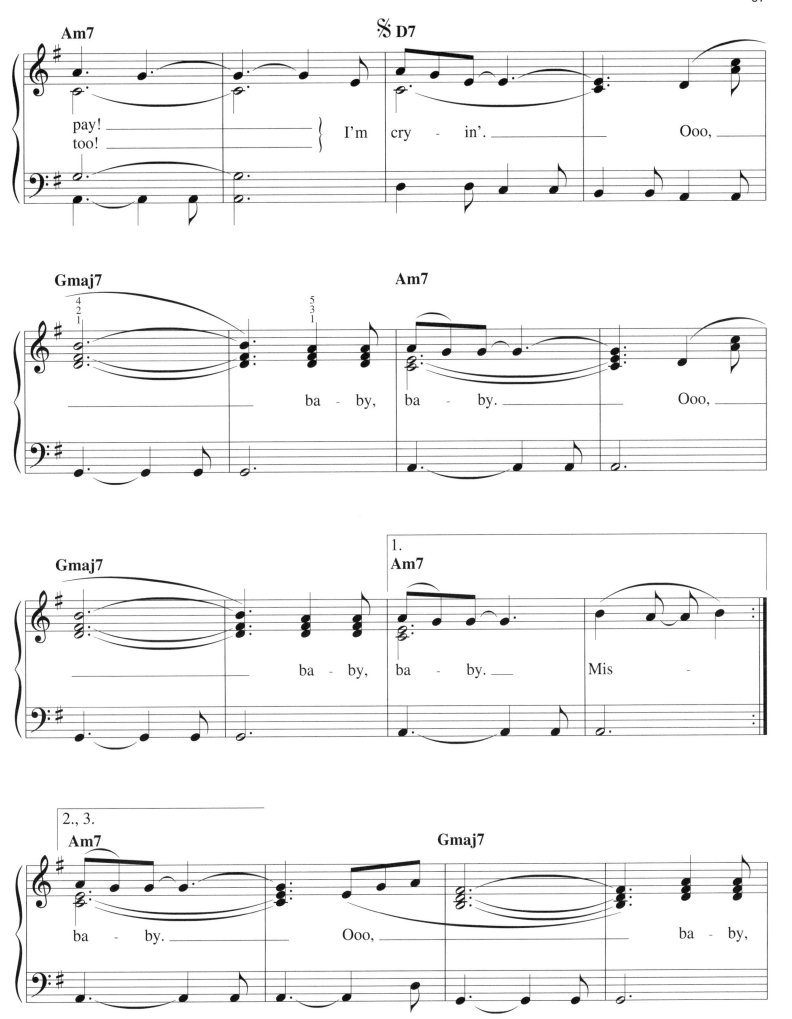

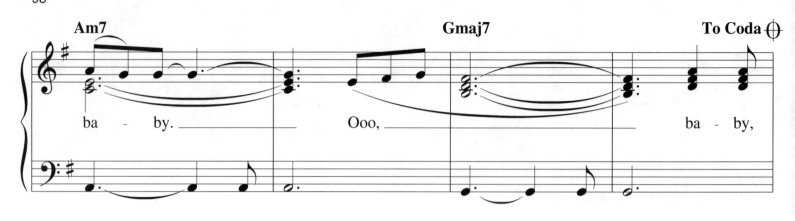

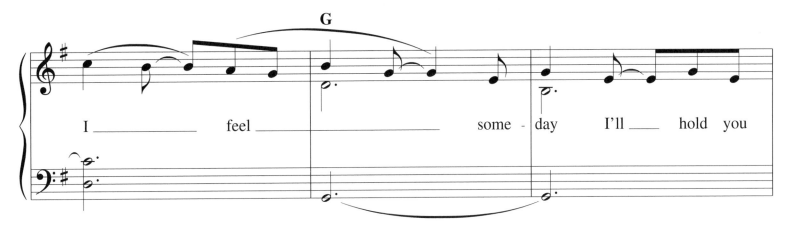

I _____ feel _____ some - day I'll ___ hold you

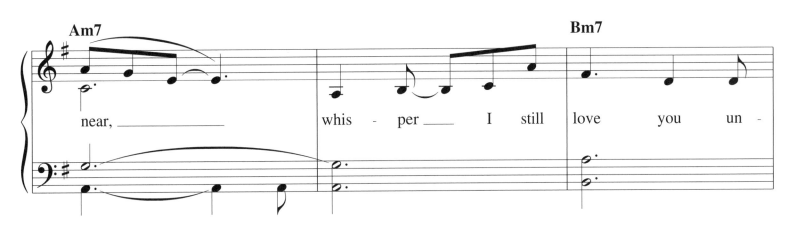

near, _____ whis - per ___ I still love you un -

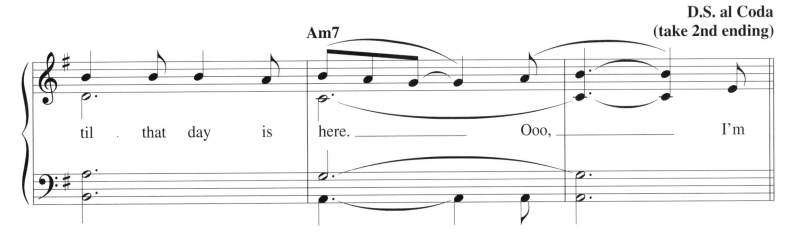

til that day is here. _____ Ooo, _____ I'm

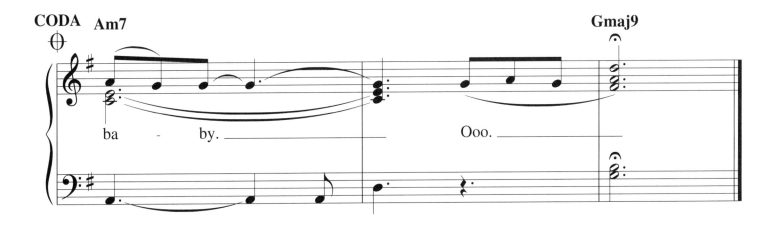

ba - by. _____ Ooo. _____

SIGNED, SEALED, DELIVERED I'M YOURS

Words and Music by STEVIE WONDER, SYREETA WRIGHT,
LEE GARRETT and LULA MAE HARDAWAY

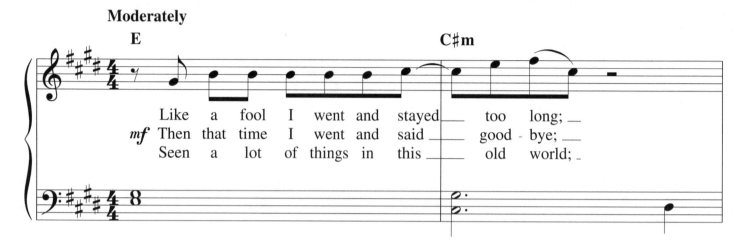

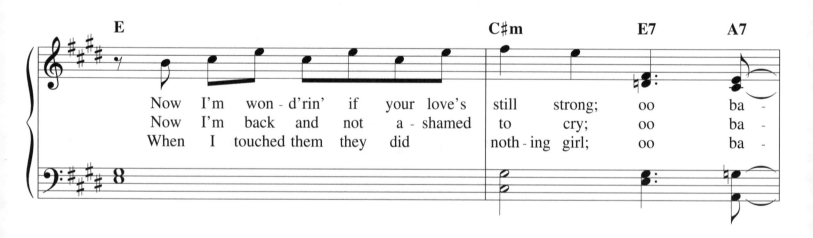

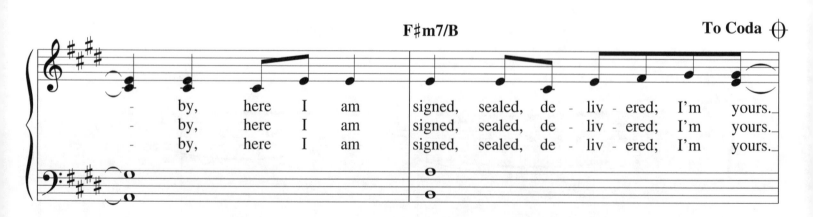

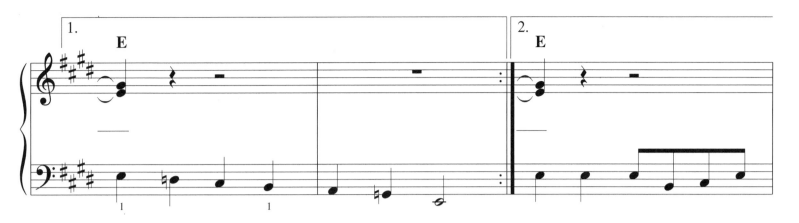

Here I am, ba - by,

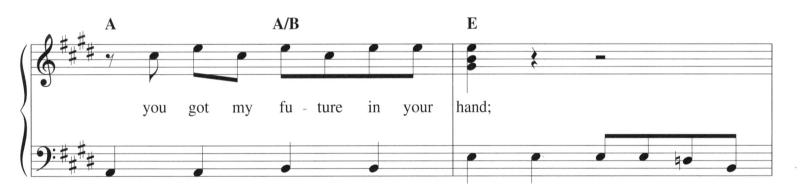

you got my fu - ture in your hand;

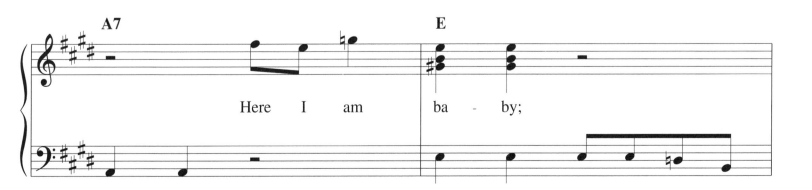

Here I am ba - by;

you got my fu - ture in your hands.

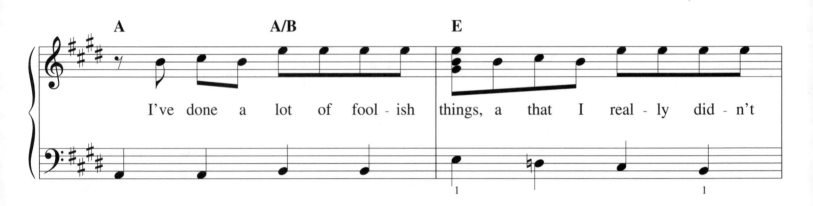

I've done a lot of fool - ish things, a that I real - ly did - n't

D.C. al Coda

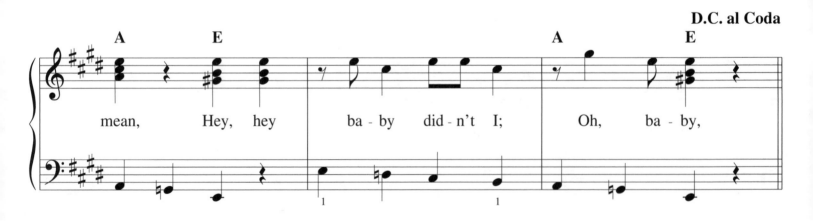

mean, Hey, hey ba - by did - n't I; Oh, ba - by,

CODA

STOP! IN THE NAME OF LOVE

Words and Music by LAMONT DOZIER,
BRIAN HOLLAND and EDWARD HOLLAND

Moving and steady

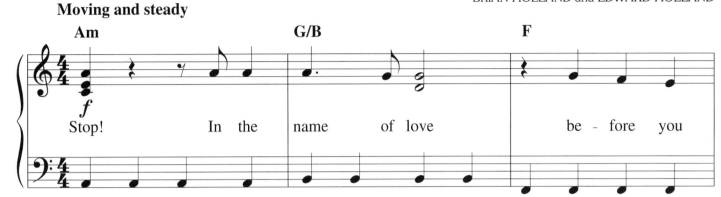

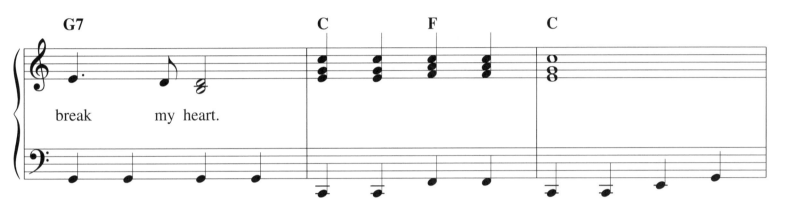

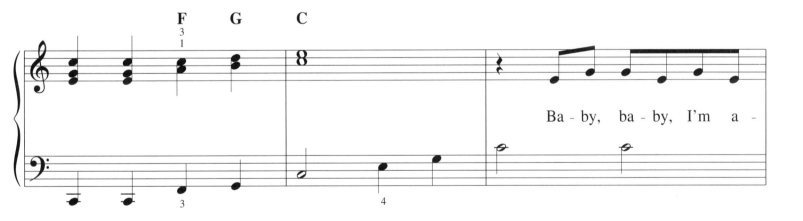

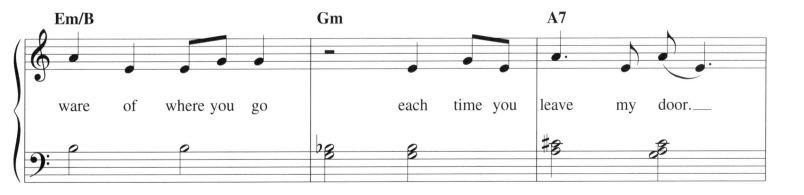

I watch you walk down the street, know - ing your oth - er

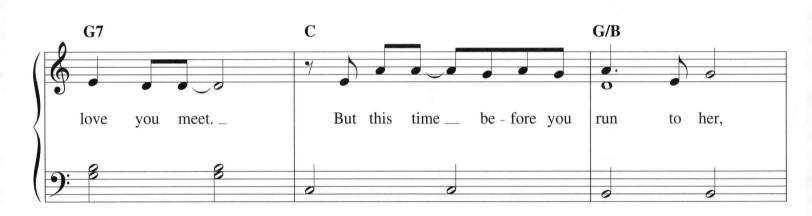

love you meet. _ But this time _ be - fore you run to her,

leav - ing me a - lone _ to cry... Have-n't I been

good to you? ____ Have-n't I been sweet _ to you? _

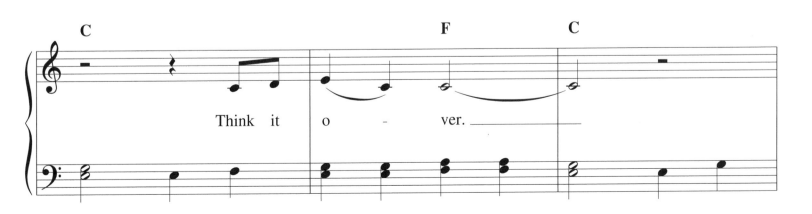

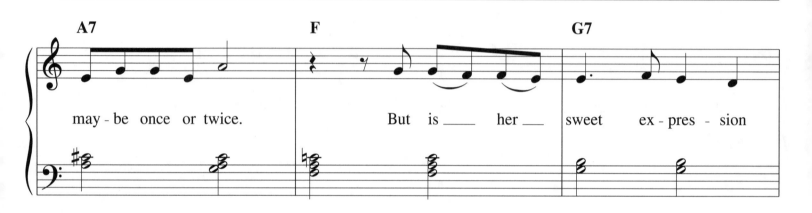

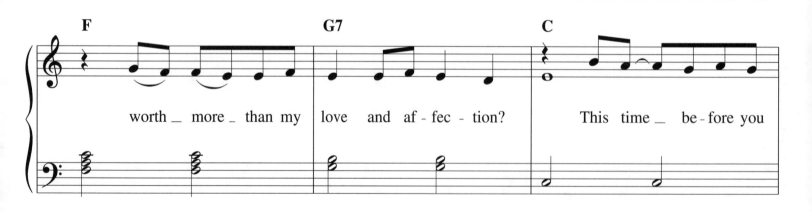

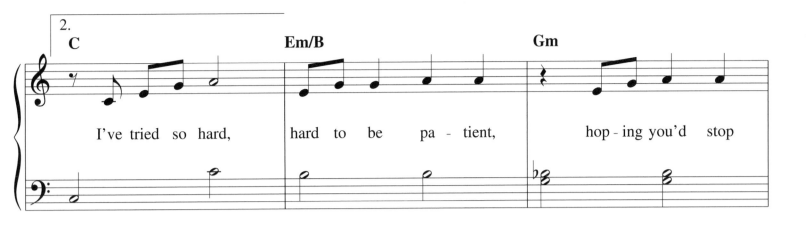

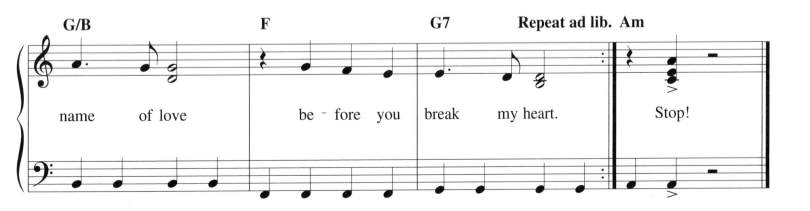

SIR DUKE

Words and Music by
STEVIE WONDER

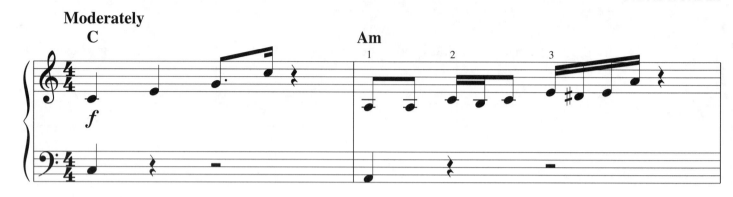

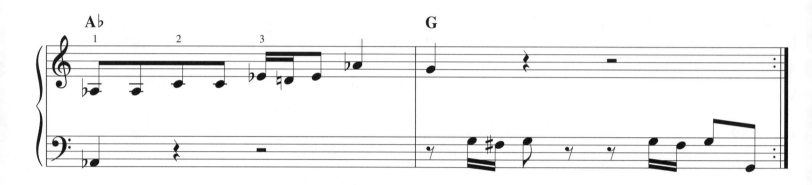

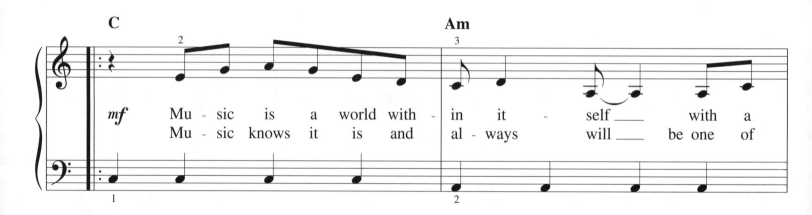

Music is a world with - in it - self ___ with a
Music knows it is and al - ways will ___ be one of

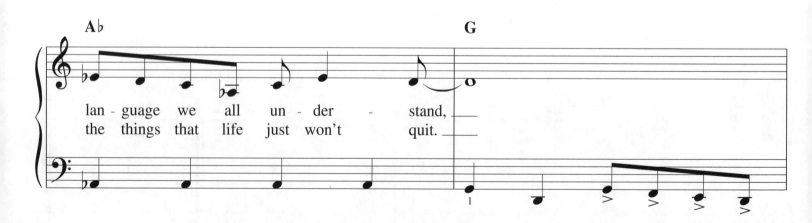

lan - guage we all un - der - stand, ___
the things that life just won't quit. ___

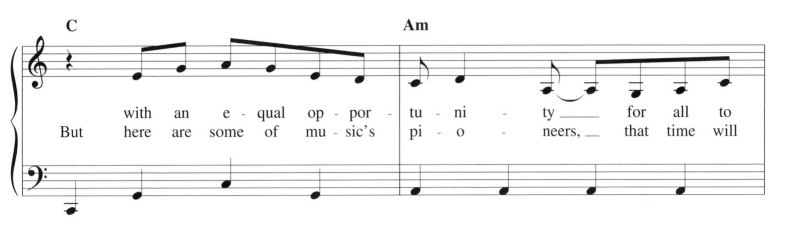

with an e - qual op - por - tu - ni - ty _____ for all to
But here are some of mu - sic's pi - o - neers, ___ that time will

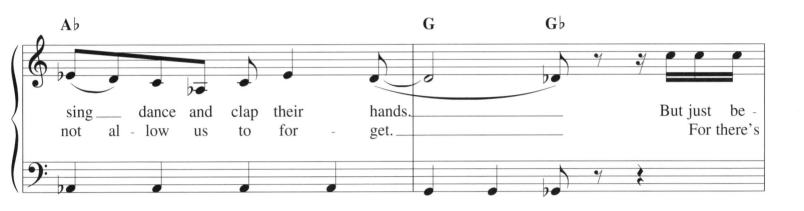

sing ___ dance and clap their hands. _____ But just be -
not al - low us to for - get. _____ For there's

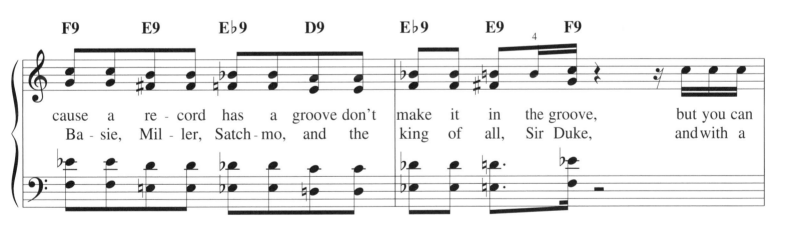

cause a re - cord has a groove don't make it in the groove, but you can
Ba - sie, Mil - ler, Satch - mo, and the king of all, Sir Duke, and with a

tell right a - way at let - ter A when the peo - ple start to move. }
voice like El - la's ring - in' out there's no way the band can lose. }

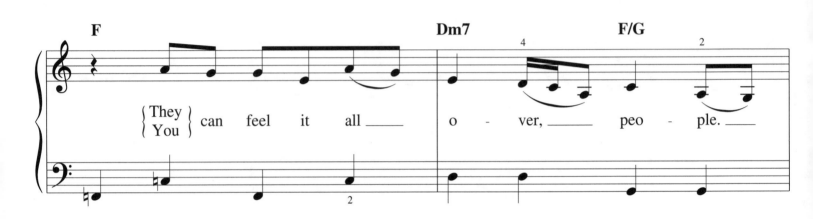

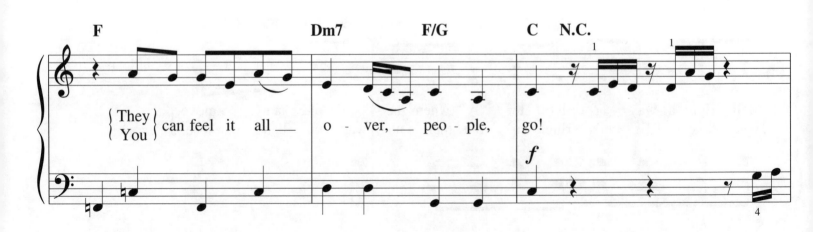

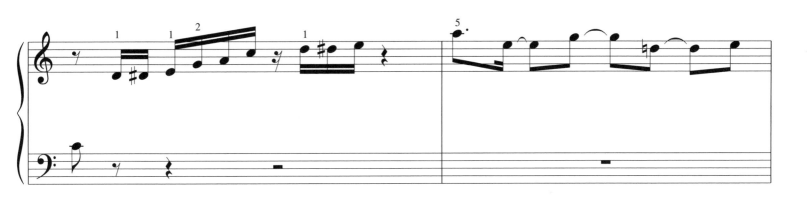

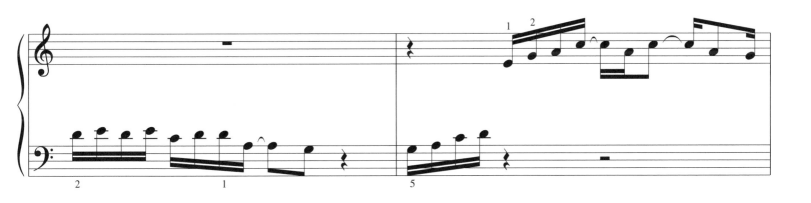

STANDING IN THE SHADOWS OF LOVE

Words and Music by EDWARD HOLLAND,
LAMONT DOZIER and BRIAN HOLLAND

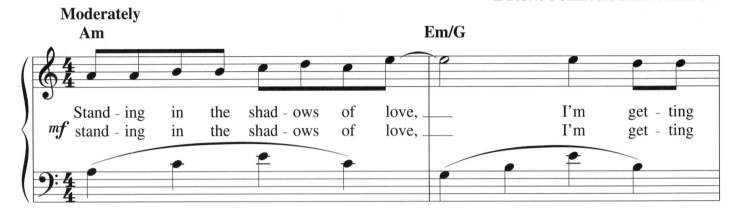

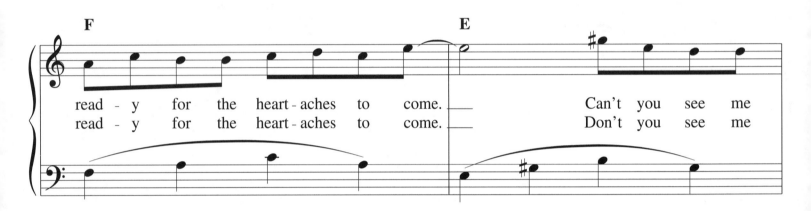

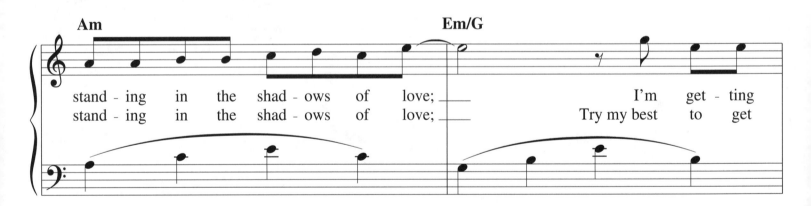

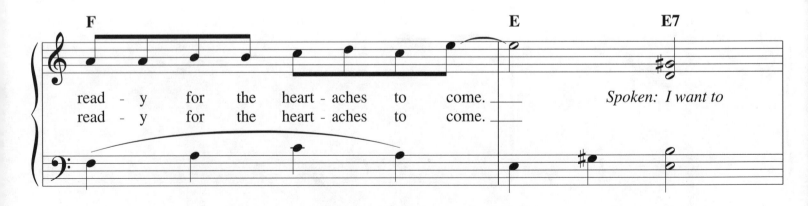

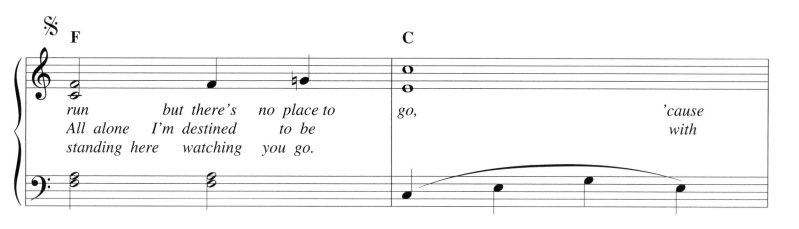

run   but there's   no place to   go,   'cause
All alone   I'm destined   to be   with
standing here   watching   you go.

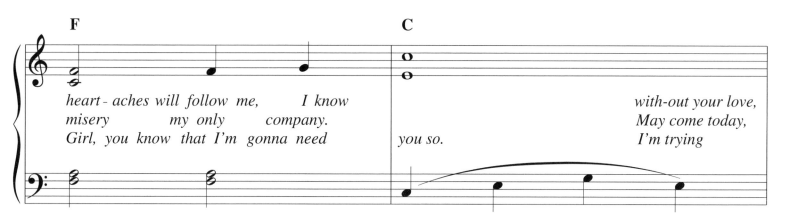

heart-aches will follow me,   I know   with-out your love,
misery   my only   company.   May come today,
Girl, you know that I'm gonna need   you so.   I'm trying

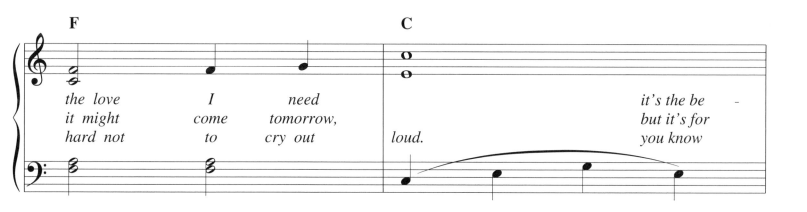

the love   I   need   it's the be -
it might   come   tomorrow,   but it's for
hard not   to   cry out   loud.   you know

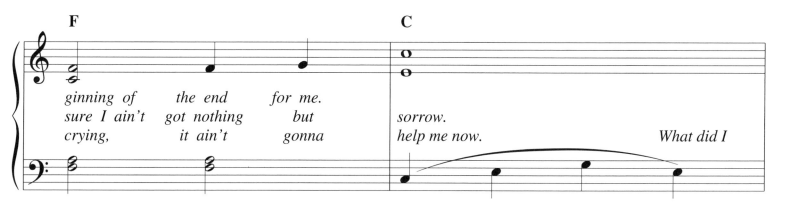

ginning of   the end   for me.
sure I ain't got nothing   but   sorrow.
crying,   it ain't   gonna   help me now.   What did I

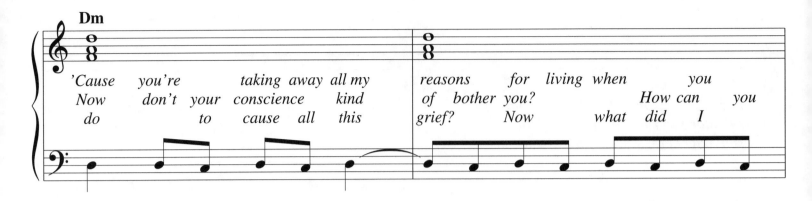

Dm

'Cause you're taking away all my
Now don't your conscience kind
do to cause all this

reasons for living when you
of bother you? How can you
grief? Now what did I

A   **B♭dim**   **To Coda** ⊕

pushed a - side all the love I been
watch me cry after all I done for
say to make you want to

giving, now wait a minute.
you. Hold on a minute.
leave, now wait a minute.

Am

Sung:
Didn't I treat you right, now ba - by, didn't I?
Gave you all the love I had now, didn't I?

When

1.

Didn't I do the best I could now, didn't I? So don't you leave me
you needed me me I was al - ways there now,

wasn't I? *Spoken:* I'm

Gave my heart and soul to you now,

didn't I? And

didn't I al - ways treat you good, now

didn't I?

STILL

Words and Music by
LIONEL RICHIE

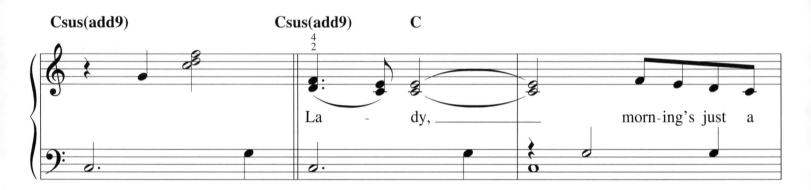

Lady, _____ morn-ing's just a

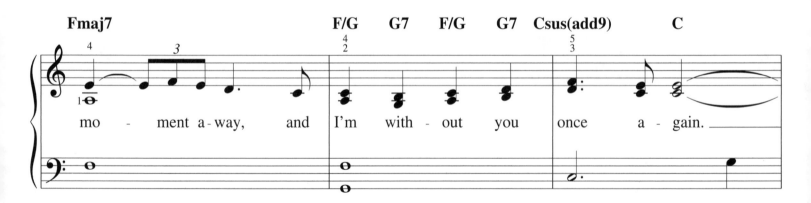

mo - ment a - way, and I'm with - out you once a - gain. _____

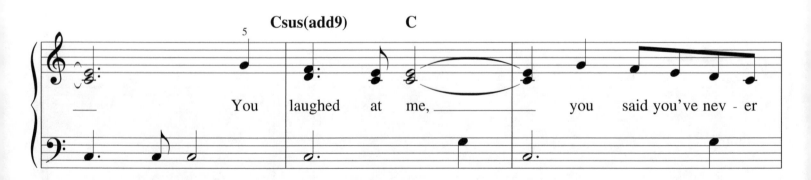

_____ You laughed at me, _____ you said you've nev - er

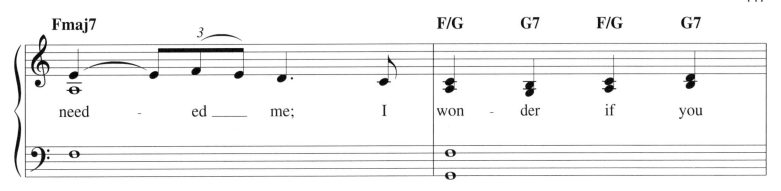

need - ed ___ me; I won - der if you

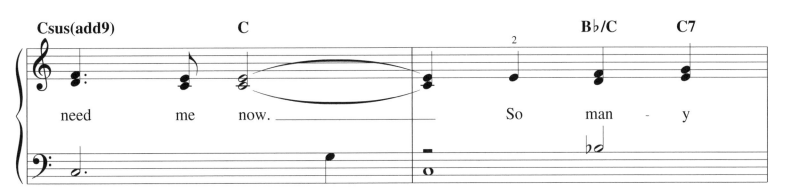

need me now. ___ So man - y

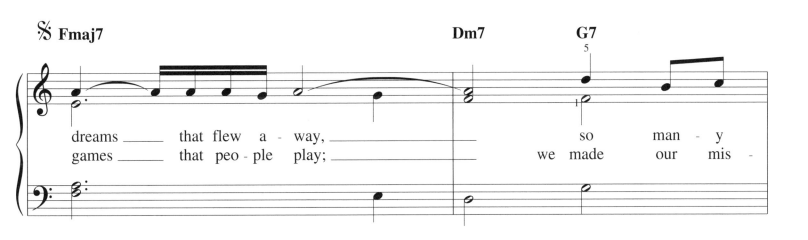

dreams ___ that flew a - way, ___ so man - y
games ___ that peo - ple play; ___ we made our mis -

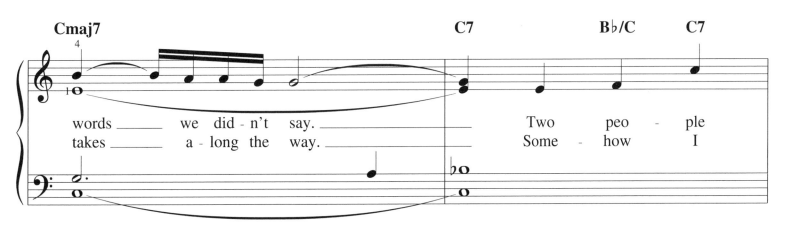

words ___ we did-n't say. ___ Two peo - ple
takes ___ a - long the way. ___ Some - how I

lost in a storm, _____ where did we go, where'd we
know deep in my heart _____ you need - ed me, 'cause I

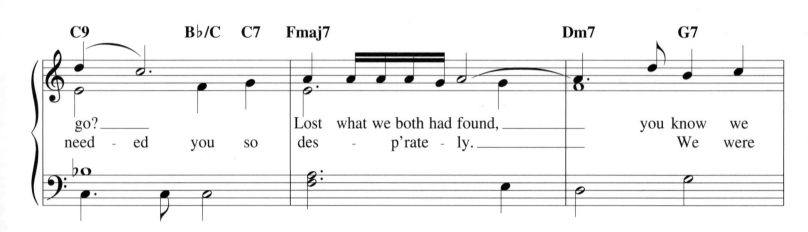

go? _____ need - ed you so des - p'rate - ly. _____

Lost what we both had found, _____ you know we
We were

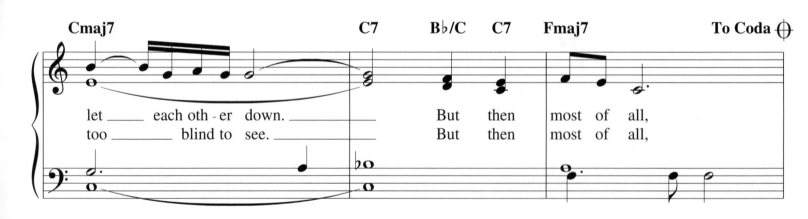

let _____ each oth - er down. _____ But then most of all,
too _____ blind to see. _____ But then most of all,

I do love _____ you still. _____

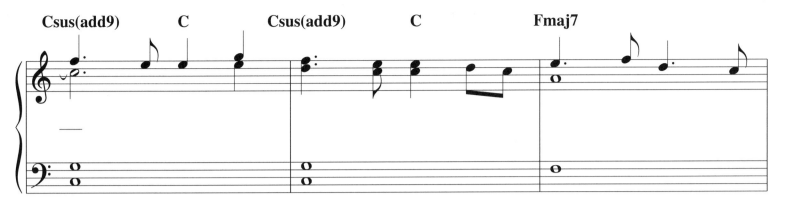

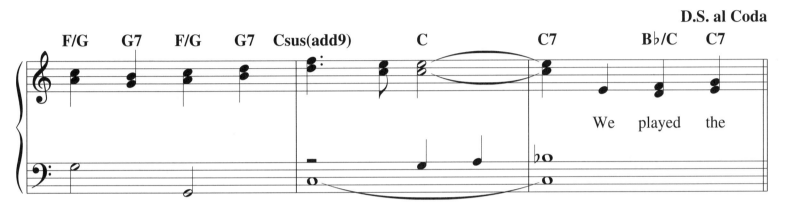

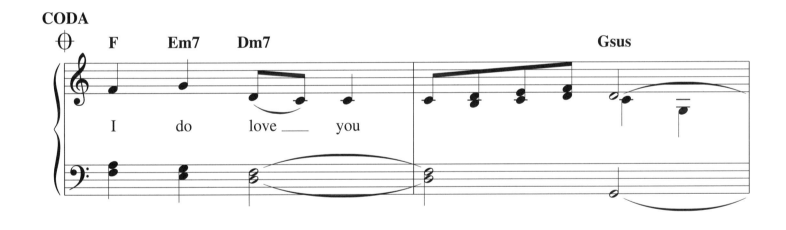

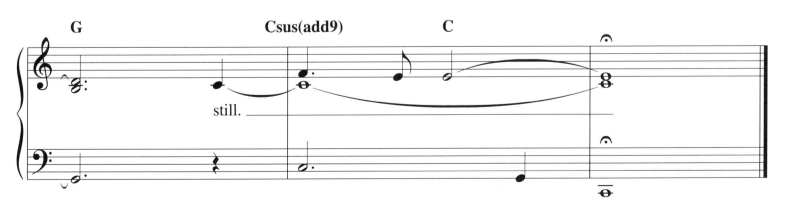

SUPERSTITION

Words and Music by
STEVIE WONDER

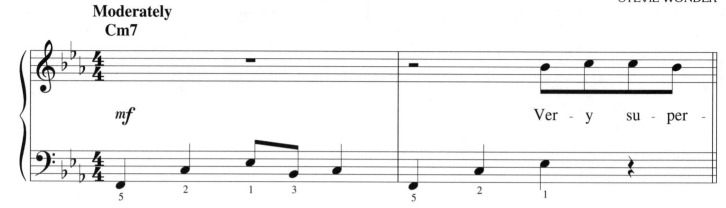

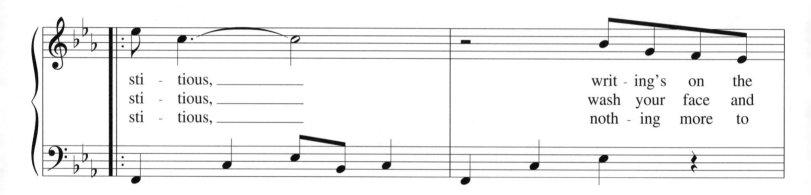

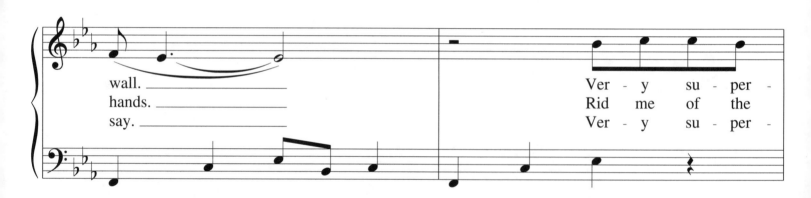

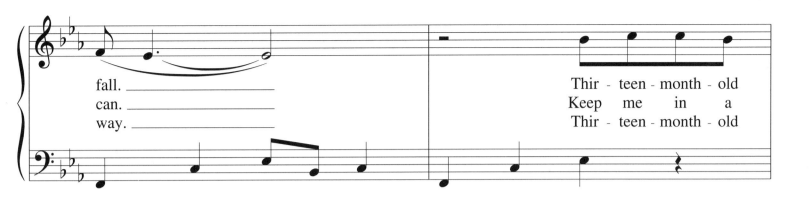

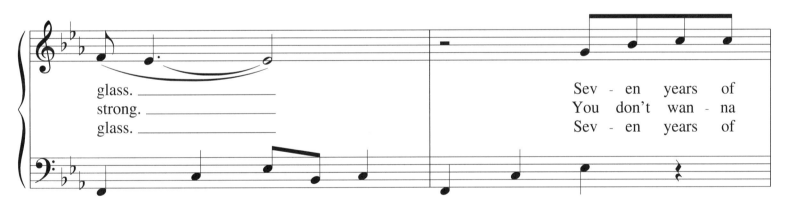

When you be-lieve ___ in things that you don't

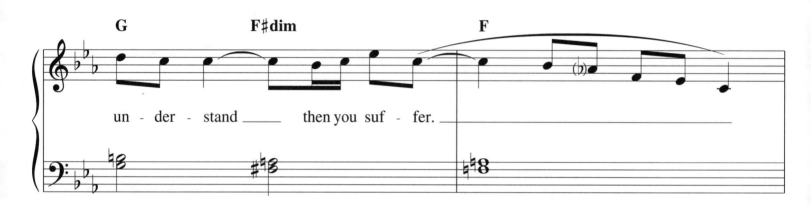

un - der - stand ___ then you suf - fer. ___

Su-per-sti-tion ain't the way. ___

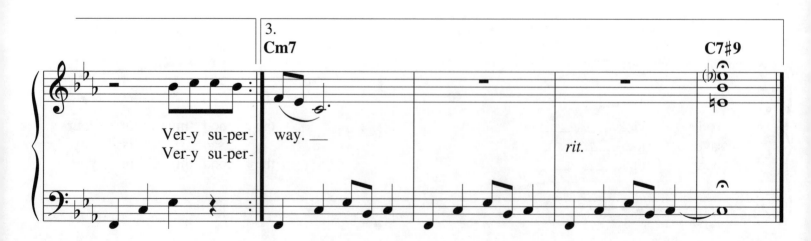

Ver-y su-per- way. ___
Ver-y su-per-

rit.

THREE TIMES A LADY

Words and Music by
LIONEL RICHIE

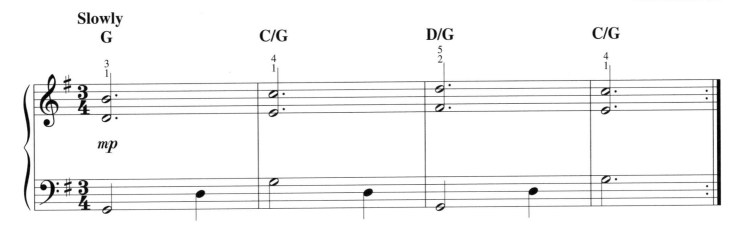

Thanks for the times that you've giv - en me. ___ The

mem - 'ries are all in ___ my mind. ___ And

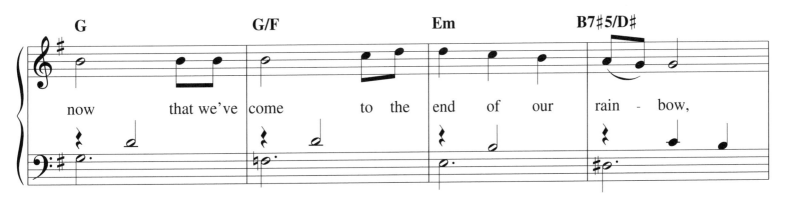

now that we've come to the end of our rain - bow,

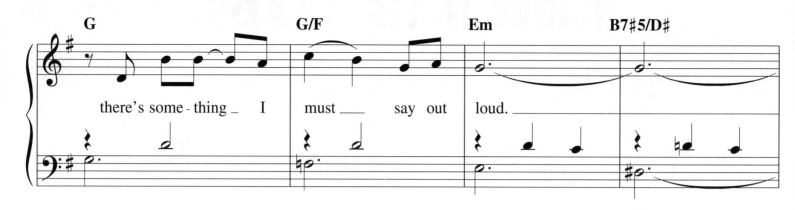

there's some-thing _ I must _ say out loud. _

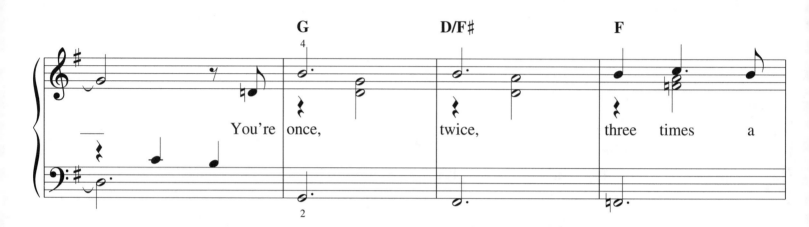

_ You're once, twice, three times a

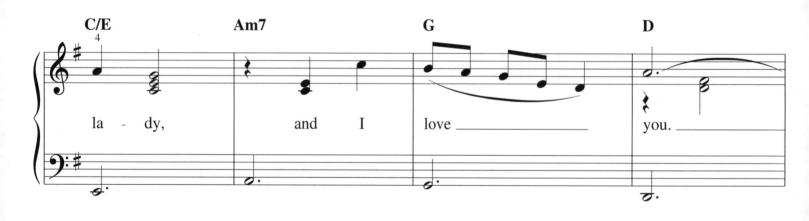

la - dy, and I love _____ you. _

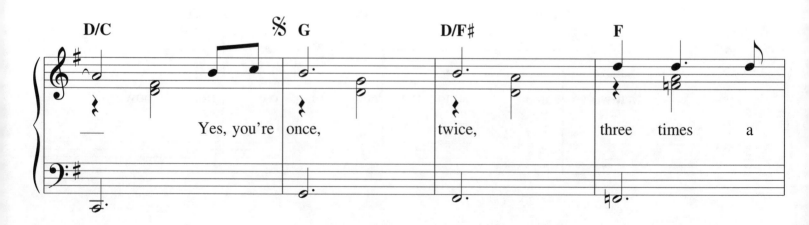

_ Yes, you're once, twice, three times a

la - dy, and I love _____ you, _____

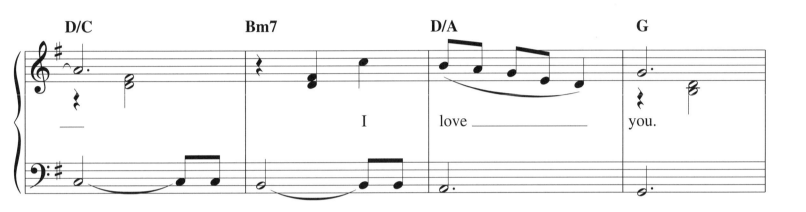

_____ I love _____ you.

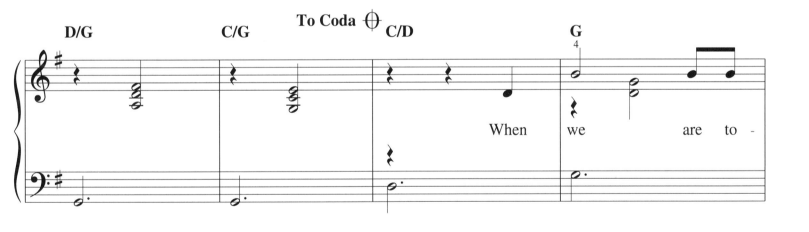

To Coda When we are to -

geth - er, the mo - ments I cher - ish with ev - 'ry

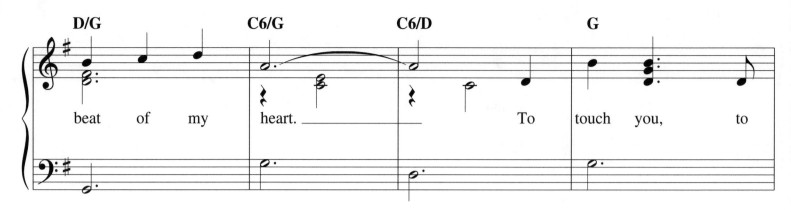

beat   of   my   heart. _____   To   touch   you,   to

hold   you,   to   feel   you,   to   need   you;   there's   noth - ing   to

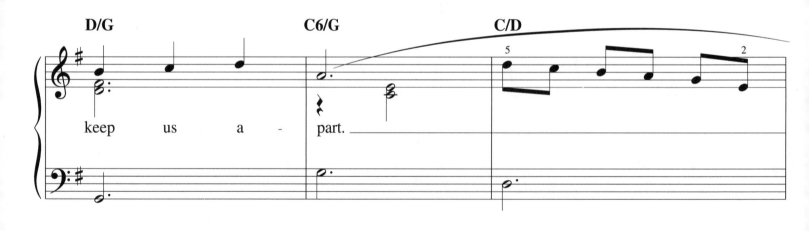

keep   us   a - part. _____

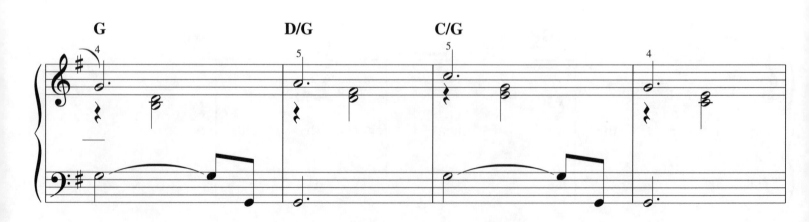

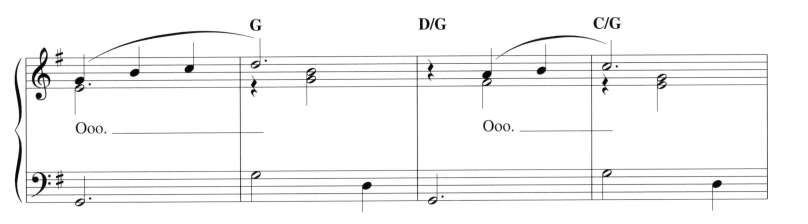

Ooo. _____ Ooo. _____

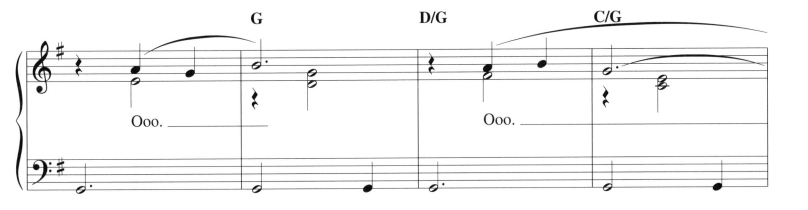

Ooo. _____ Ooo. _____

D.S. al Coda

CODA

You're

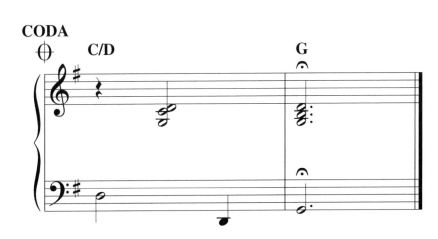

WHERE DID OUR LOVE GO

Words and Music by BRIAN HOLLAND,
LAMONT DOZIER and EDWARD HOLLAND

Moderately

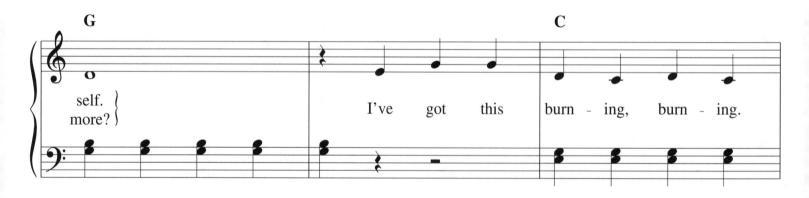

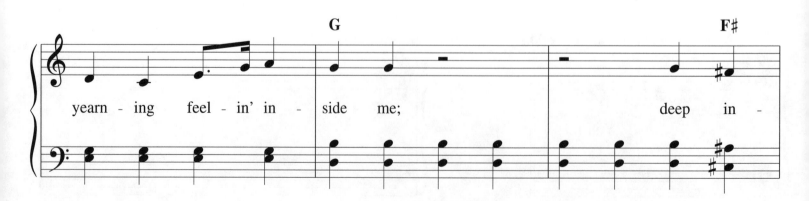

side me; and it hurts so bad.

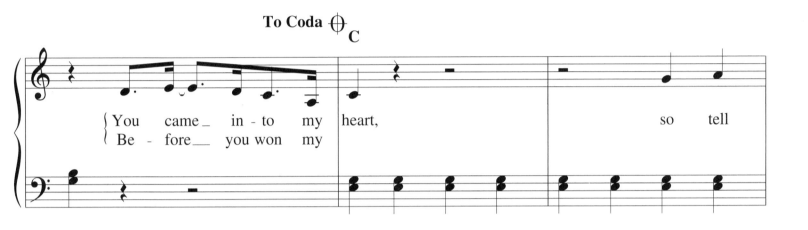

You came — in - to my heart, so tell
Be - fore — you won my

me _____ with a burn - ing love

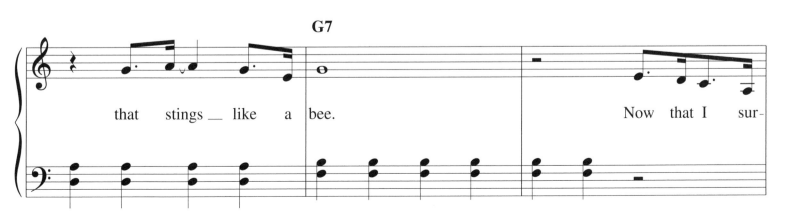

that stings __ like a bee. Now that I sur-

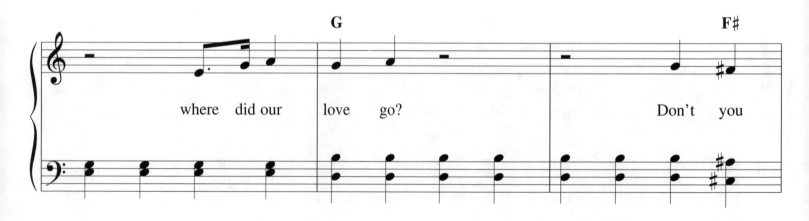

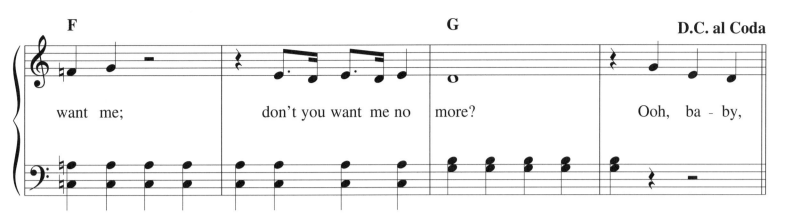

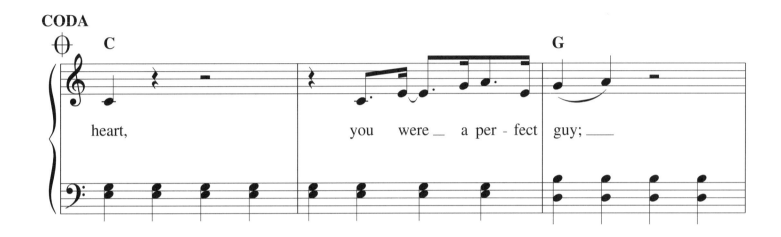

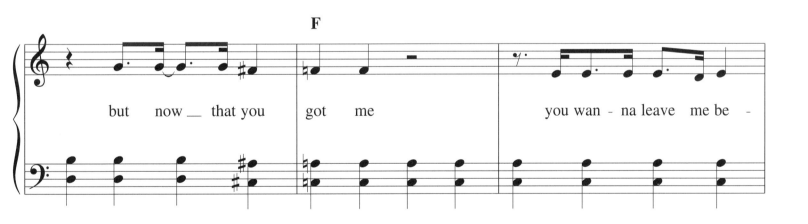

YOU ARE THE SUNSHINE OF MY LIFE

Words and Music by
STEVIE WONDER

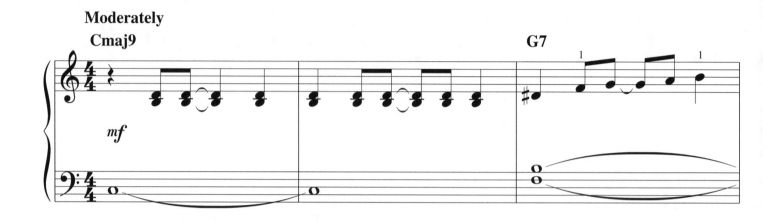

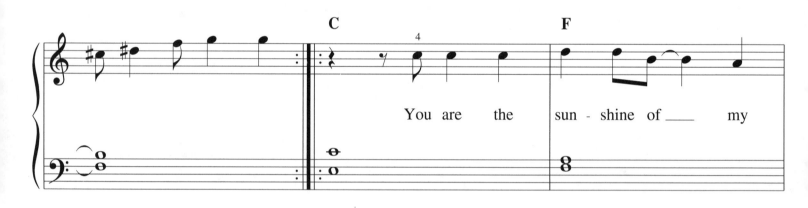

You are the sun - shine of ____ my

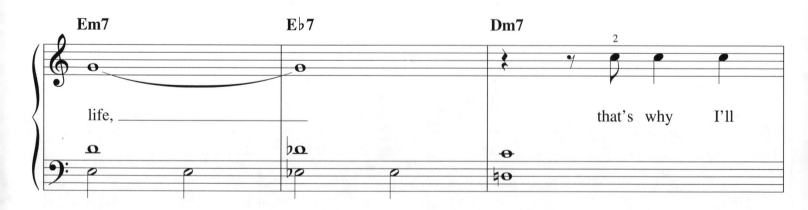

life, ____ that's why I'll

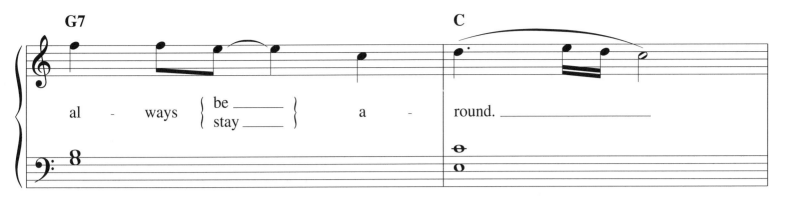

al - ways { be _____ / stay _____ } a - round. _____

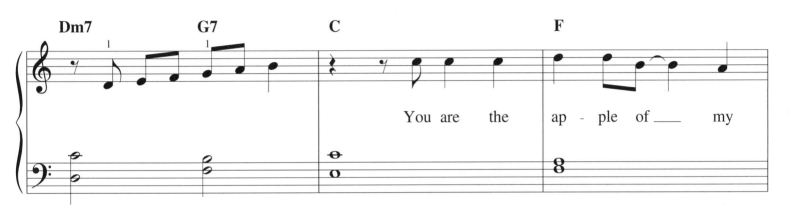

You are the ap - ple of ___ my

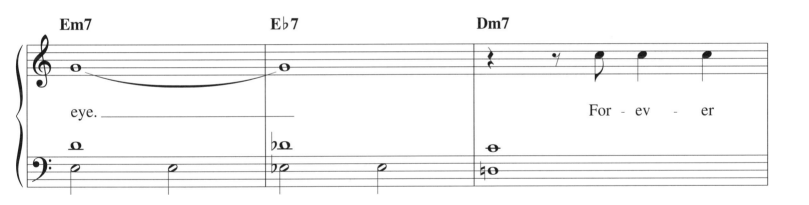

eye. _____ For - ev - er

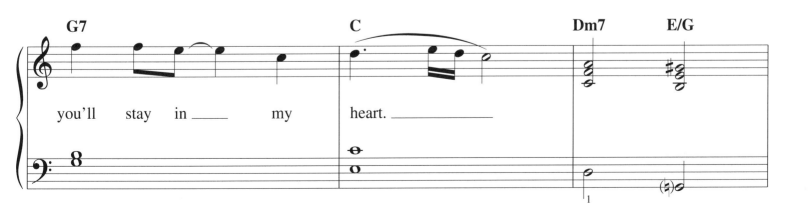

you'll stay in _____ my heart. _____

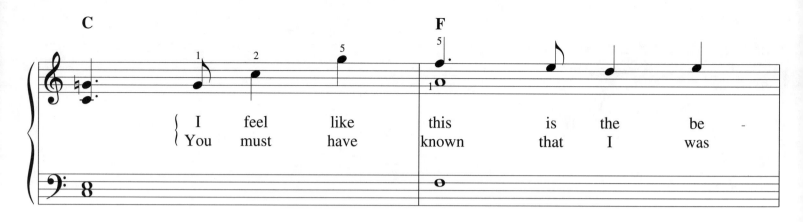

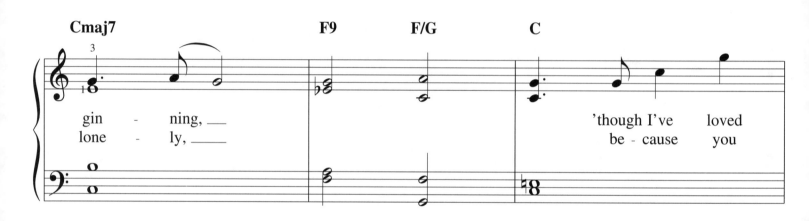

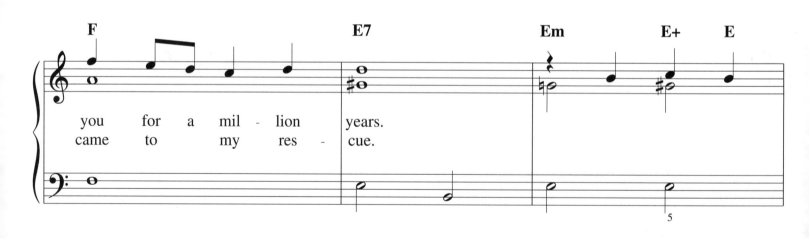

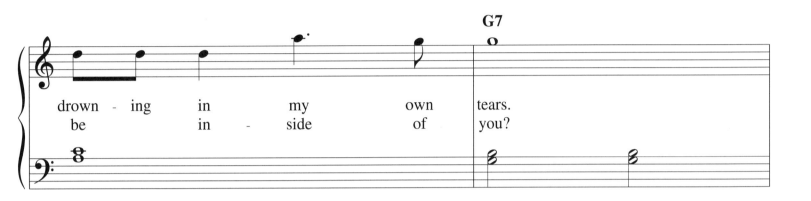

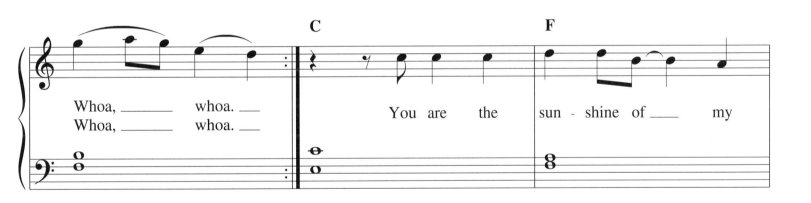

YOU KEEP ME HANGIN' ON

Words and Music by EDWARD HOLLAND,
LAMONT DOZIER and BRIAN HOLLAND

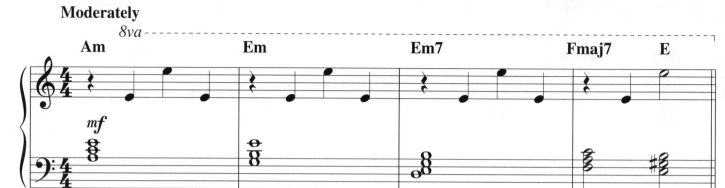

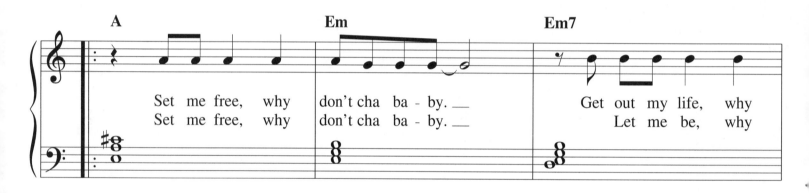

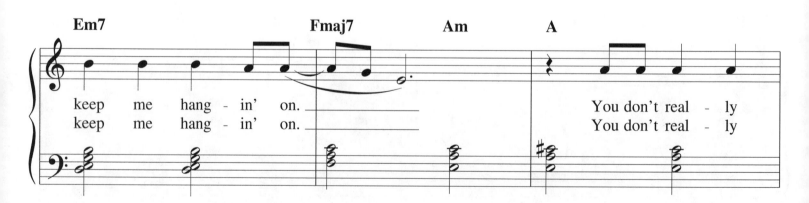

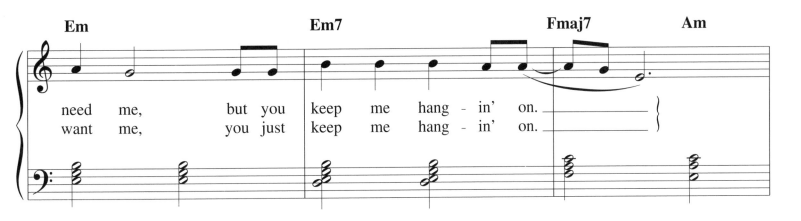

need me, but you keep me hang - in' on. ____

want me, you just keep me hang - in' on. ____

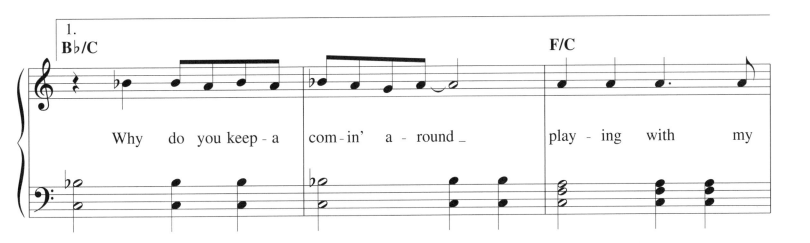

1.

Why do you keep-a com - in' a - round ____ play - ing with my

heart? ____ Why don't cha get out of my life ____

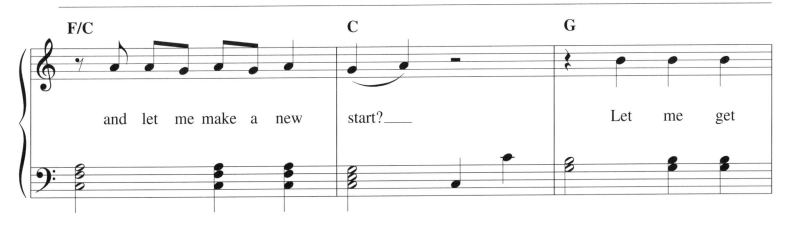

and let me make a new start? ____ Let me get

o - ver you ___ the way you've got - ten o - ver me. ___

2.

You say ___ al - though ___ we ___ broke up ___ you still wan - na be just

friends. But how can we still ___ be friends ___ when see - ing you on - ly breaks my

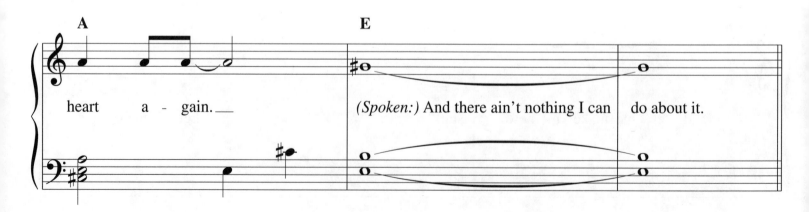

heart a - gain. ___ *(Spoken:)* And there ain't nothing I can do about it.

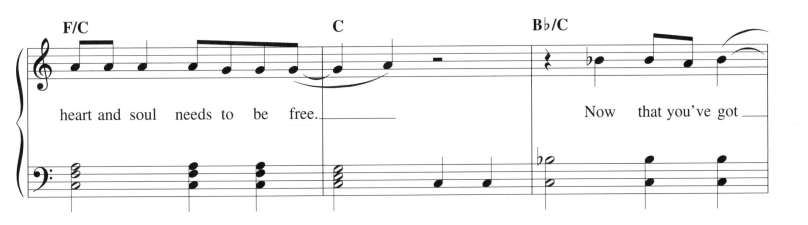

You don't want me for your-self ___ so let me find some-bod - y else.

___ Why don't _ cha be a man a - bout ___ it

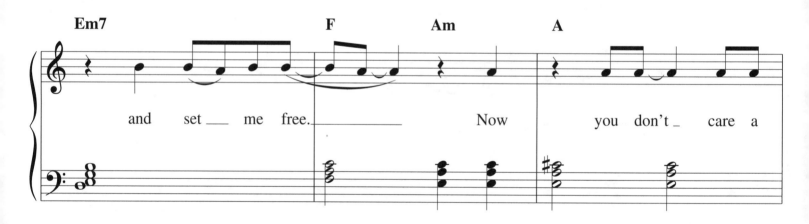

and set ___ me free. ___ Now you don't _ care a

thing a - bout me. ___ You're just us - ing me. ___ Boy,

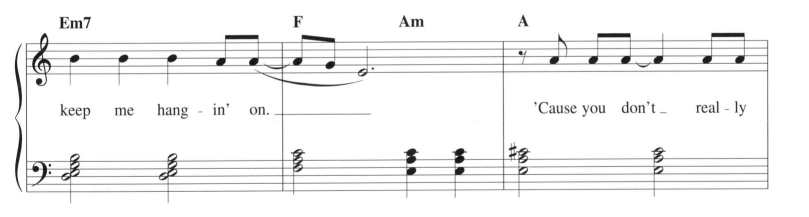

THE TRACKS OF MY TEARS

Words and Music by WILLIAM "SMOKEY" ROBINSON,
WARREN MOORE and MARVIN TARPLIN

Moderately

Peo - ple say I'm the life of the par - ty 'cause
Since you left me if you see me with an - oth - er girl

I tell a joke or two.
seem - ing like I'm hav-ing fun,

Al - though I
Al - though she

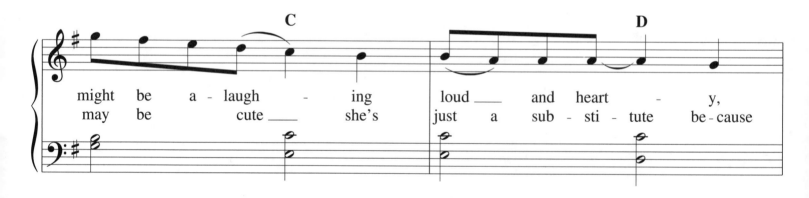

might be a - laugh - ing
may be cute she's

loud and heart - y,
just a sub - sti - tute be - cause

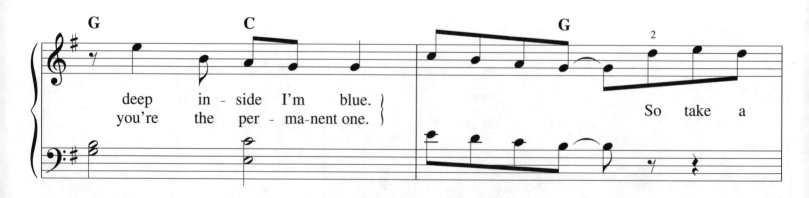

deep in - side I'm blue.
you're the per - ma-nent one.

So take a

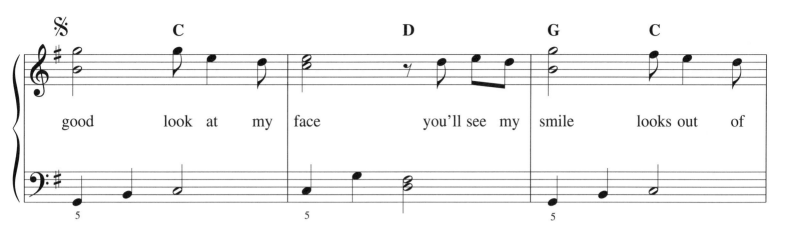

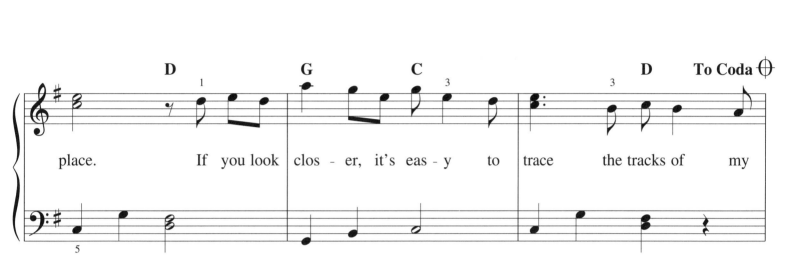

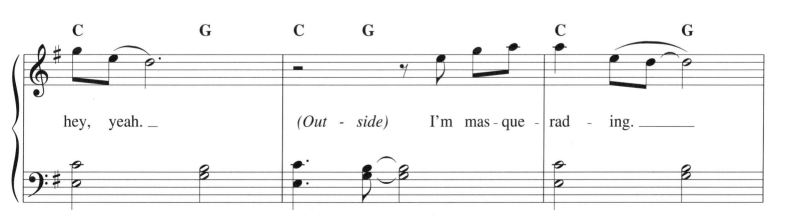

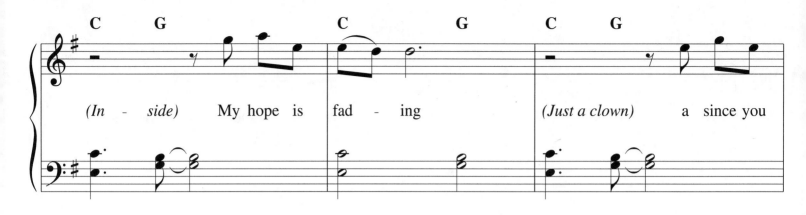

(In - side) My hope is fad - ing (Just a clown) a since you

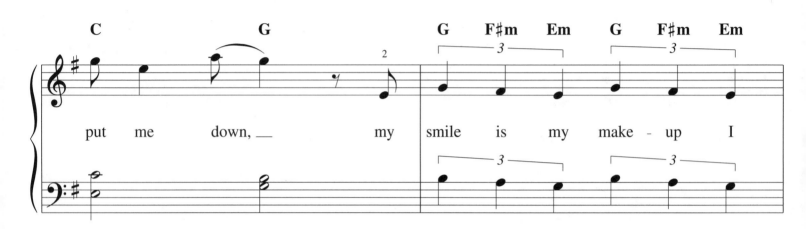

put me down, __ my smile is my make - up I

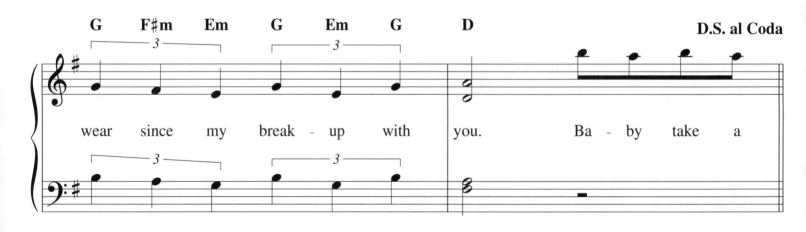

wear since my break - up with you. Ba - by take a

D.S. al Coda

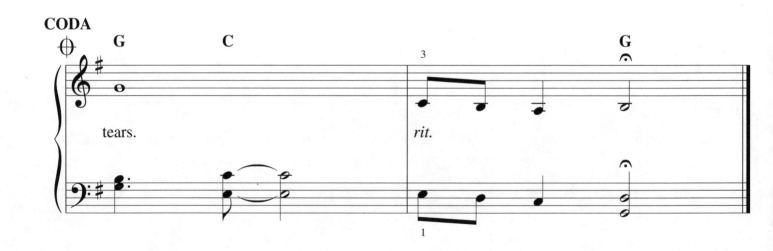

CODA

tears. *rit.*